theatre & ireland

Theatre&
Series Editors: Jen Harvie and Dan Rebellato

Published
Colette Conroy: *Theatre & the Body*
Jill Dolan: *Theatre & Sexuality*
Helen Freshwater: *Theatre & Audience*
Jen Harvie: *Theatre & the City*
Nadine Holdsworth: *Theatre & Nation*
Erin Hurley: *Theatre & Feeling*
Joe Kelleher: *Theatre & Politics*
Ric Knowles: *Theatre & Interculturalism*
Helen Nicholson: *Theatre & Education*
Lionel Pilkington: *Theatre & Ireland*
Paul Rae: *Theatre & Human Rights*
Dan Rebellato: *Theatre & Globalization*
Nicholas Ridout: *Theatre & Ethics*

Forthcoming
Joel Anderson: *Theatre & Photography*
Dominic Johnson: *Theatre & the Visual*
Caoimhe McAvinchey: *Theatre & Prison*
Bruce McConachie: *Theatre & the Mind*
Juliet Rufford: *Theatre & Architecture*
Rebecca Schneider: *Theatre & History*

Theatre&
Series Standing Order: ISBN 978–0–230–20327–3 paperback

You can receive further titles in this series as they are published by placing a standing order. Please contact your bookseller or, in the case of difficulty, write to us at the address below with your name and address, the title of the series, and the ISBN quoted above.

Customer Services Department, Palgrave Macmillan Ltd.
Houndmills, Basingstoke, Hampshire, RG21 6XS, England

theatre & ireland

Lionel Pilkington

palgrave
macmillan

First published 2010 by
PALGRAVE MACMILLAN

Palgrave Macmillan in the UK is an imprint of Macmillan
Publishers Limited, registered in England, company number
785998, of Houndmills, Basingstoke, Hampshire RG21 6XS.

Palgrave Macmillan in the US is a division of St Martin's Press LLC,
175 Fifth Avenue, New York, NY 10010.

Palgrave Macmillan is the global academic imprint of the above
companies and has companies and representatives throughout
the world.

Palgrave® and Macmillan® are registered trademarks in the United
States, the United Kingdom, Europe and other countries.

ISBN 978–0–230–57462–5   paperback

This book is printed on paper suitable for recycling and made
from fully managed and sustained forest sources. Logging,
pulping and manufacturing processes are expected to conform to
the environmental regulations of the country of origin.

A catalogue record for this book is available from the British
Library.

A catalog record for this book is available from the Library of
Congress.

Printed and bound in China

contents

series editors' preface

The theatre is everywhere, from entertainment districts to the fringes, from the rituals of government to the ceremony of the courtroom, from the spectacle of the sporting arena to the theatres of war. Across these many forms stretches a theatrical continuum through which cultures both assert and question themselves.

Theatre has been around for thousands of years, and the ways we study it have changed decisively. It's no longer enough to limit our attention to the canon of Western dramatic literature. Theatre has taken its place within a broad spectrum of performance, connecting it with the wider forces of ritual and revolt that thread through so many spheres of human culture. In turn, this has helped make connections across disciplines; over the past fifty years, theatre and performance have been deployed as key metaphors and practices with which to rethink gender, economics, war, language, the fine arts, culture and one's sense of self.

Theatre & is a long series of short books which hopes to capture the restless interdisciplinary energy of theatre and performance. Each book explores connections between theatre and some aspect of the wider world, asking how the theatre might illuminate the world and how the world might illuminate the theatre. Each book is written by a leading theatre scholar and represents the cutting edge of critical thinking in the discipline.

We have been mindful, however, that the philosophical and theoretical complexity of much contemporary academic writing can act as a barrier to a wider readership. A key aim for these books is that they should all be readable in one sitting by anyone with a curiosity about the subject. The books are challenging, pugnacious, visionary sometimes and, above all, clear. We hope you enjoy them.

Jen Harvie and Dan Rebellato

foreword

Some years ago I attended a luncheon in the City of London at which the Mayor praised the business community for its success in exporting to Ireland. Replying, the Irish Minister could not resist mentioning the shameful export of Irish corn to Britain during the Irish famine. He further retaliated by listing Ireland's *cultural* exports to Britain – Congreve, Sheridan, Wilde, Shaw and Beckett. Like much-needed myths, these playwrights functioned as a psychic defence for all that was missing in the fledgling Irish Republic. They marked the British theatre indelibly by seemingly portraying that dominant society from the inside, while actually looking from without.

In this book Lionel tracks with great clarity the complexity of Irish buffoonery, national theatricality and dissent. The Revolution led Yeats and Lady Gregory to banish the old folksy foolishness of the Irish identity by flagging up the need for an Irish renaissance. The flag is a signifier – what we do with the territory after securing independence is the issue. I have read this book as a performer and tried to see the consequences of its argument in that light.

Under Yeats a speedy phenomenon of the writing of plays and the application of naturalism in performance followed, but it remained the dominant style even after the methods of acting and writing changed elsewhere. Naturalism is a type of acting that aims to imitate life. In Ireland such imitation is full of traits that emulate eccentricities of behaviour of the oppressed. As this book reveals, the Irish are theatrical in their daily lives: the accents of districts, extremes of foolishness, drunkenness, terror and barbarism are all reflected in our humour. It was on such a diet that I was brought up – the turns of phrase and sounds of the near-hysteria of exclamation, a diet of downtrodden women and drunken men. Humour became ossified, formalised on stage, at odds with the myth of the land of saints and scholars, but brilliantly turned on its head later. The poetry of a country systematically hunted since the Poynings Law in 1494 which changed Irish ways to English ways and the punch-drunk centuries of Penal laws, has become folded into a deconstructed version by our contemporary writers. As Lionel shows, with the invention of theatrical Ireland – all half-doors and mad women on boglands – however surreal, the performances have remained in the domestic.

I remember the excitement in 1982 when Druid Theatre Company brought *The Playboy of the Western World* to the Edinburgh Festival and suddenly a lid was off in performance. The traditional folk showcase was gone, and we were released into a new form of self-image that revealed barbaric, atavistic temperaments. The play suddenly had significance outside the island. Ireland was joining Europe as a self-investigating grown-up.

Now the post revolution century is nearly up and we are on the brink of new challenges. Our great actors like Donal Mccann never did take on the big European classical roles instead bringing a classical dimension to contemporary plays. I found when I went to play Hedda Gabler in Dublin, the gasps at her suicide showed that the audience did not know the play, a classic in Europe was new for Ireland.

These are exciting times. Never has there been a more pertinent moment than now, as the Church, which siphoned off the imagination of many, collapses under its own self-delusion, along with our financial stability. Irish theatre and its actors have the opportunity to shape the future by looking outwards; there are needs that go beyond naturalism and behaviourism. A poetic scale of performance makes the actor rise and meet the language with the spatiality of a stage that does not mimic the domestic. An expression of feeling does not have to be infused with the restriction of oppression. And the understandable resistance to plays written during the English Renaissance is now obsolete. Shakespeare and the Jacobeans, those architects of Western European drama, have yet to make a significant re-entry into audiences' consciousness, and our unusual slant could make these plays another device to refract the multifariousness of our diversity.

This is the next phase – yet to be enjoyed in Ireland. I hope that with the new plan to train Irish actors towards this broadened repertoire, we will produce performances that match the huge writing talent offered by Murphy, McGuinness and Carr. With actors who have a seam of the European classical tradition, we will expand our dimension, making us more translatable to an audience outside Ireland and moving forward our own view of ourselves in relation to the ever-widening world.

theatre & ireland

Introduction

Why write a book about theatre *and* Ireland? What is it about Ireland that warrants this special attention? Why (one might ask) in a series of books committed to exploring theatre's *conceptual* relationships should the island of Ireland be singled out for consideration? Why not Wales, or the West Indies, or any other country or region that one might think of? And what does a book about theatre and Ireland tell us about either Ireland or theatre?

For students of English literature and drama familiar with names such as Oliver Goldsmith, George Farquhar, Richard Brinsley Sheridan, W. B. Yeats, George Bernard Shaw, J. M. Synge, Sean O'Casey, Teresa Deevy, Samuel Beckett, Brian Friel, Tom Murphy and Marina Carr, the answer may seem obvious, even pedestrian: Ireland is home to a disproportionately large number of well-known dramatists. If you glance at recent Tony Award nominations (www.

tonyawards.com/en_US/archive/ceremonies/index.html)
or at the number of Irish plays performed in London, New
York, Toronto and Sydney, it is also clear that as far as mainstream international English-speaking theatre is concerned,
Ireland continues to be responsible for high numbers of contemporary plays and playwrights. Moreover, Irish theatre
tends to evoke associations that are positive and reassuring.
Read the newspaper headline 'New Irish Play' and in all
likelihood the article below will be a story of rejuvenation,
eloquence and excitement. What the English critic Kenneth
Tynan wrote in 1956 – 'It is Ireland's sacred duty to send
over, every few years, a playwright to save the English theatre from inarticulate dumbness' (quoted in Nicholas Grene's
Politics of Irish Drama, 1999, p. 262) – could be said to be
true of most decades of the twentieth century or, indeed,
of any recent century. And let's not forget either that amazing 1990s upbeat tap-dancing spectacular *Riverdance: The
Show*, with its sexed-up version of Irish dancing performed
at record-breaking speed. All in all, and within the context
of English-speaking theatre especially, Ireland has a far from
ordinary historical importance.

But there are related, and to my mind more interesting,
reasons that the topic of theatre and Ireland is worthy of
consideration. For many centuries Ireland and things Irish
have been viewed as essentially performative: as possess-
ing a core of being that is inherently theatrical. There is
our much-loved propensity for charm and flattering exag-
geration, known as 'blarney', and a less charming but just as
enduring reputation for deviousness and verbal chicanery.

And then there is the brogue, a heavy Irish accent that is so obviously emphatic – so deviant and ludic in relation to the norms of English pronunciation and therefore so potentially replete with solecisms – that it appears to be something performed.

Performativity is also suggested by the oxymorons that are sometimes produced when the word 'Irish' is deployed as an adjective. The *Oxford English Dictionary*, for example, defines 'Irish confetti' as meaning sticks, stones and other such injury-making missiles and an 'Irish bridge' as an open stone drain carrying water across a road. And an Irish coffee, of course, is just the thing for intoxicating your sobriety, or sobering up your intoxication. In these examples, the word 'Irish' does rather more than modify the nouns that it precedes. It theatricalises them: it suffuses them with a logic that is histrionic, extraordinary, the very opposite of what might be expected. In her 2007 article 'Comely Maidens and Celtic Tigers', performance critic Aoife Monks remarks that 'Irish' has another and more recent usage: as a verb. Monks argues that when the word 'Irish' is used in this way, as it was in a 2001 episode of *The Simpsons* when Ned Flanders' newly acquired show-girl wife asked him 'to Irish up' a cup of coffee, what is envisioned is not just an addition (add whiskey and stir) but 'an action, a practice ... even perhaps, a performance' (p. 1).

Looked at from yet another perspective, Matthew Arnold's famous nineteenth-century diagnosis of the Celtic temperament in 'On the Study of Celtic Literature' as involving a 'rebellion against fact' and 'straining human nature further than it will stand' (1867, pp. 64–65) could be taken just as well as a description of the art of an actor. This facility for acting has been much commented on. 'The Catholic community gives us some of our best actors and actresses derived chiefly from Gaelic stock', writes one mid-twentieth-century commentator from Northern Ireland; 'its people take naturally to the theatre' (David Kennedy, 'The Ulster Region and the Theatre', 1946, p. 51). Sometimes, though, it is the Irish as a whole who are actors: 'Ireland is a company of character actors disguised as a nation', as Clive Barnes once put it in *The New York Times* ('Critic's Notebook', 1976, p. 75). Here Barnes draws on his readers' familiarity with the comic figure of the stage Irishman (of which more later) and with the idea that being Irish means playing a part.

In addition to Ireland's reputation in historical and political texts as a location for the 'drama' of rebellion, anti-colonial insurgency and terrorist outrage, in other words, there is a perennial suggestion – spread out over several centuries and to be found in multifarious cultural documents – that Ireland possesses the raw materials for theatre (actors, histrionics, a performative use of language) without the proper means to produce theatre. 'We have been living through real dramas', lamented one national theatre advocate in 1895, 'and have no time for dramas of the imagination' (W. Barrett, 'Irish Drama', p. 40).

Such deeply held cultural assumptions help explain why the setting up of a national theatre in Ireland in the late nineteenth and early twentieth centuries is so often viewed as a cultural watershed and as unequivocally liberationist. Indeed, for some commentators Irish drama *begins* with this national theatre movement, and with the 1904 establishment of the Abbey Theatre. For many of its contemporary supporters as well, a national theatre was supposed to demonstrate that Ireland had become modern and that it had moved away from the disruptive militancy of anti-colonial violence and insurgency. Ireland's national theatre was institutional proof that the country had moved beyond an era of sporadic, insurrectionary and sometimes revolutionary acts and that it now accepted the disciplinary norms of representative democracy. Establishing a national theatre institution in Ireland, in other words, was not just about providing a forum for the performance of Irish plays. It was about demonstrating and normalising an idea of politics based on constitutional representation. Democracy was normalised not as revolutionary change and popular empowerment but as a more constrained process of a people delegating power to political representatives. With its illuminated stage, darkened auditorium, naturalistic acting and – notionally at least – deferentially attentive audience, the theatre presented itself as a model for an ideal society. 'In the theatre', Yeats wrote in 1899, 'a mob becomes a people' ('The Irish Literary Theatre' [1975], p. 141).

One other effect of this longstanding association of Ireland with the histrionic is that the theatre in and for Ireland is viewed as an improving cultural phenomenon that is crucial to the country's development and particularly well suited for the expression of the often-wayward performativity of its people. This view of theatre as a modernising institution dominates the field of Irish theatre studies. Mostly unchallenged in the critical literature, it gives rise to a way of thinking about the history of Irish theatre as a developmental and improving cultural narrative. As we shall see, this forward-looking story parallels the history of colonialism *and* of nationalism in Ireland; it also has the effect of separating the theatre from a range of non-institutional performance practices. The sections of this book on theatre history and on non-institutional theatre in Ireland discuss these ideas in more detail.

I believe that the longstanding association of Ireland and performance is deeply connected to the country's experience of colonialism and that this is the frame within which the Irish theatre is best understood. For a colonising power (and, as we shall see, for postcolonial state-sponsored nationalisms as well), the disquieting differences and demands that are presented by the political, social and cultural life of the dispossessed are acknowledged, and yet simultaneously registered as subordinate and unimportant, when the dispossessed themselves are viewed as innately histrionic. For its colonisers, Ireland's apparent theatricality delegitimises the country's resistance to colonialism. Viewing Irish actions and the capacity for violent or militant anticolonial resistance as blundering, blustering and belligerent performances, of course, can operate both as a reassurance to the coloniser or postcolonial elite and as an impetus for resolute military action and repression. By the same token, in the post-independence Ireland of the 1920s Sean O'Casey's representation of the Dublin lower orders as colourfully histrionic does not leave audiences excessively disturbed about issues of urban poverty and deprivation. The comic routines and malapropisms of Boyle and Joxer in the first act of *Juno and the Paycock* (Abbey Theatre, Dublin, 1924) or Fluther's entertaining Dublin vernacular in *The Plough and the Stars* (Abbey Theatre, Dublin, 1926) exhibit these characters' obliviousness to their poverty and help to absolve the audience of political responsibility for it. Thinking of a class, ethnic group or nationality as innately performative tends to make light of its economic circumstances and of its political demands. Viewed as a performance, in other words, the seriousness of any action is undermined by a double stigma: that it is really only pretence and that it is a form of self-enjoyment. But performative actions are not always reassuring, and the extravagant theatricality of O'Casey's characters is also mordantly subversive of the Catholic and middle-class pieties of the Irish state. As we shall see in relation to the figure of the stage Irishman, the idea that the colonised subject is also a performer often functions in a manner that is profoundly unsettling for the coloniser, and for postcolonial elites.

Finally, in Ireland and outside Ireland, Irish drama has come to be associated, over several centuries, with a process of confirming the modernity of its audience. In his 1999 study of Irish theatre from Dion Boucicault to Brian Friel, *The Politics of Irish Drama*, Nicholas Grene observes that 'Ireland in the Irish play is a world elsewhere' (p. 262). Grene argues that the setting of an Irish play tends to be rural (or working-class urban) and that the effect of this is to leave its spectator feeling more alert as to the reasons she or he now lives at a distance from this rural, other world on stage (p. 262). In the face of an Irish condition that is shown as generally benighted, the audience is confirmed in its contemporary, future-oriented modernity. If the theatre of Samuel Beckett offers a striking exception to this trend – fracturing, rather than consolidating, its audiences' perspectives – this is in part because Beckett refuses the idea that his plays can be characterised as representing Ireland.

The close link between Irish theatre and modernity also explains the historically close relationship between theatre and the state in Ireland and, more latterly, between theatre and big business. It explains why in 1925 – at a time when the Irish Free State (as Ireland was then called) had reduced the old age pension and was cutting back on social expenditure in general – Ireland became the first English-speaking country to offer a state subsidy for its national theatre. The theatre, it was thought, would help push Ireland forward into the modern. What worked out in practice was more complex, varied and disruptive.

The association of theatre in Ireland with modernisation also sheds light on the ways in which the strategies of big business and much mainstream Irish theatre are now deeply entwined in a project to present Ireland as a recognisable 'brand', as Patrick Lonergan points out in his 2009 book *Theatre and Globalization: Irish Drama in the Celtic Tiger Era* (pp. 188–89). Attempts by the Irish government to 'sell Ireland' abroad (that is, to attract foreign direct investment) often entail presenting potential investors with a theatrical production (p. 22). This is not merely incidental. Selling Ireland favours Irish theatre because theatre conveys a performativity that not only is viewed as memorably and essentially Irish but also serves as an exemplary demonstration of our Irish ability to conform to what others want. The 'natural' performativity exhibited by Irish theatre demonstrates Ireland's renowned Celtic Tiger ability to adjust, adapt and remake itself according to the volatile demands of fast-track global capitalism. Dominant though it may be, this is not the only way in which Ireland's 'performativity' functions in relation to contemporary capitalism. As we shall see, the idea of an intrinsic theatricality implies that the structures governing current social, political and economic norms are provisional and unfixed and that our understandings of performance and politics are closely related. These ideas are discussed in more detail in the book's concluding section, on modernity.

Overall, therefore, this book argues that to understand the relationship between theatre and Ireland it is not enough to study theatrical representation as it takes place within the institutional theatre. Theatre *in* Ireland is a cultural phenomenon that is not restricted to professional, urban, building-based theatre. What this means in practice is that any discussion of plays presented on the Irish stage cannot be separated from consideration of these plays' relationship to alternative and competing traditions of popular drama and performance or, indeed, from consideration of other contemporary, non-institutional forms of theatrical expression or 'counter-theatre'. My argument, in short, is that the apparently innate theatricality of the Irish helps us to understand how theatre and performance work in general. It also helps us understand something about the history of Ireland as a real place and as a concept, and about the ways in which a society's cultural resources for resistance are revealed through performance. Thinking about theatre and Ireland means expanding the critical frame in which theatre is understood. As this book will argue, theatrical performance is not just the enactment of a literary script but also a playful public intervention, a testimony to the resilience of alternative ways of thinking, remembering and imagining action, and a wholesale stretching out of what a society thinks might be possible.

The stage Irishman

One enduring reason for the close association of the theatre and Ireland is the figure of the stage Irishman. As Clive Barnes' remark about Ireland as a nation of character actors reminds us, the condition of Irishness is haunted by the long history of its theatrical representation. Stage Irishmen appear in English and Irish drama from as early as the 1580s; they continue – either as definite characters or as a dramatic legacy affecting the portrayal of Irish personality – until the present. Examples of the stage Irishman are the denigrated and unnamed Irish Catholic bishop in George Peele's *Battle of Alcazar* (Rose Theatre, London, 1592), the immensely popular Teague in Richard Howard's *The Committee* (Drury Lane, London, 1662), Foigard, a duplicitous and lecherous

Catholic priest, in George Farquhar's *The Beaux' Stratagem* (Queen's Theatre, London, 1707), Conn, a lovable rogue, in Dion Boucicault's *The Shaughraun* (Wallack's Theatre, New York, 1874), the garrulous Tim Haffigan in George Bernard Shaw's *John Bull's Other Island* (Royal Court Theatre, London, 1904) and Fluther (doubling as stage working class as well as stage Irish) in Sean O'Casey's *The Plough and the Stars* (Abbey Theatre, Dublin, 1926). Legacies of the contradiction-loving stage Irishman can be discerned, for example, in the way in which J. M. Synge's *The Playboy of the Western World* (Abbey Theatre, Dublin, 1907) portrays a rural west of Ireland community responding rapturously to the revelation by the protagonist, Christy, that he has killed his father and in Tom Murphy's study of racism and violence in an Irish immigrant family living in the English town of Coventry in his play *A Whistle in the Dark* (Theatre Royal, Stratford East, London, 1961). A less sophisticated and more recent treatment of the type lies in the brutalised and vacuously comic characterisations evident in Martin McDonagh's much-lauded *The Beauty Queen of Leenane* (Town Hall Theatre, Galway, 1996) and in *The Lieutenant of Inishmore* (The Other Place, Stratford-upon-Avon, 2001).

One reaction to the stage Irishman is to condemn the figure as a racial slur and as a caricature to be rejected. It is an understandable response. Indeed, this is the nationalist and anti-colonial impulse expressed by W. B. Yeats and Lady Gregory in their prospectus for the Irish Literary Theatre (predecessor to the Abbey) in the late 1890s: 'We will show that Ireland is not the home of buffoonery and

easy sentiment, as it has been represented, but the home
of an ancient idealism' (Gregory, *Our Irish Theatre* [1972],
p. 20). There are two major problems with this response.
First, replacing a stage caricature with an idealistic alternative is not quite the revolutionary gesture that it seems.
Buffoonery or ancient idealism – what both versions have in
common is their assumption of a single fixed identity that
can be established as nationally representative and that is at
a distance from the contemporary modernity of the audience. Second, an outright rejection of the stage Irishman
overlooks some of the productive ambiguities that performing any identity on stage necessarily entails, and not least
those of an apparently feckless clown. It also overlooks many
of the creative and exploratory techniques that dramatists
such as J. M. Synge and Tom Murphy have brought to bear
on this convention.

Moreover, a stage Irishman is never just a character actor. As a performer performing, there is a built-in
element of reflexivity that resides within this convention.
Inadvertently ironic, that is, the performance of the stage
Irishman holds a powerful potential to expose some of the
anxieties and uncertainties that give rise to the stereotype in the first place. And, as we know from psycho-
therapy, the act of making uncertainty and anxiety visible
often offers a far more enduring challenge to the damaging
effects of an imposed identity than any simple rejection.
Sometimes the stage Irishman is not just a character
for an audience to laugh at but a device that makes us
think again about what makes us laugh. What I mean by

this can be illustrated by reference to one of the earliest and most frequently cited examples of a stage Irishman: Captain Macmorris in William Shakespeare's *Henry V* (Globe Theatre, London, 1599, or Court of King James, London, 1605). In Act 3, when the Welsh captain Fluellen addresses his Irish counterpart and refers in passing to 'your nation', Macmorris responds at once with an outburst of tetchy belligerence:

> FLUELLEN: Captain Macmorris, I think, look you, under your correction, there is not many of your nation —
> MACMORRIS: Of my nation? What ish my nation? Who talks of my nation? Ish a villain, and a bastard, and a knave, and a rascal? What ish my nation? Who talks of my nation?
>
> (*Henry V*, 3.3.121–26)

Macmorris' angry response seems quite disproportionate to Fluellen's perfectly civil query: 'I think, look you, under your correction'. There is also a puzzling ambiguity as to whether 'villain', 'bastard', 'knave' and 'rascal' refer to Fluellen or to Macmorris' own view of how his Irishness is perceived. One effect of this ambiguity is that Macmorris' nation — Ireland — is presented as another version of Macmorris himself: a state of mind that is volatile, belligerent and villainous. For the audience, the overall effect of Macmorris' outburst is to convey the same impression twice over. In other words, the impression of Irishness that Macmorris would have communicated to the play's Elizabethan audience confirms what the audience thought it already knew and therefore fully expected to see. In this regard, it is interesting to note that in the folio edition of *Henry V* Macmorris is referred to by a simple speech prefix: 'Irish' (Stephen O'Neill, *Staging Ireland*, 2007, p. 151). Like the stage Irishman in general, Macmorris is never just himself: he is an assigned identity conjured up by a perception of Irishness as a whole. Just as the folio edition of *Henry V* describes the part, Macmorris is another name for 'Irish'. This is exactly the way colonial stereotypes work. Confronted by the prospect of a culture that appears different to the point of being incomprehensible or simply incommensurate, a colonial stereotype sets out to soothe and reassure the coloniser that everything about this other culture can be condensed into a single point: it is inferior.

In the short exchange between Macmorris and Fluellen that we have just considered, the audience has no idea why Macmorris becomes so upset and angry. The emotions that Macmorris expresses seem far, far in excess of their apparent motivation. This behaviour is histrionic. Psychologically, something is going on that we don't know about; to this extent, the action seems exaggerated and performed. All that we do know is that Macmorris displays a recognisably Irish way of pronouncing the letter 's' ('What ish my nation?') and that his extraordinary defensiveness has been triggered by the word 'nation'. You could say that our not knowing what it is that motivates Macmorris' reaction is precisely the point. This is someone who is not worth knowing or understanding – someone who is *innately* belligerent, volatile, spoiling for a fight.

And yet this is a scene that leaves the audience feeling slightly uneasy. Thinking about it (as Stephen O'Neill's brilliant recent analysis of this scene shows), an Elizabethan audience may well have been troubled by the fact that the name Macmorris suggests not the fixed identity of Irish barbarism but an identity associated with those earlier English colonists who had integrated into the world of Gaelic Ireland and were known as 'old English'. This is suggested by the way in which the first part of the name is Irish ('Mac') and the second part is Anglo-Norman ('Morris') and by the fact that Macmorris is fighting for the English. He is an English soldier not an Irish one. Macmorris may be behaving like the native Irish, but his name, rank and military allegiance suggest that he is also closely related to the world of the play's English Elizabethan audience. More troubling again is our realisation that Macmorris' anger is directed at precisely the sort of dismissive stereotyping through which we the audience are inclined to interpret his behaviour. Macmorris, one could argue, is reacting to the identity that Fluellen and the audience insist on assigning to Ireland, *and* he is also a product of that identity. In terms of the colonial stereotype of the stage Irishman there is something about Macmorris, then, that is so far from reassuring that it threatens to reactivate and even exacerbate the uncertainties about suppressing a conquered people that imposing the stereotype in the first place is designed to dispel and allay. Belligerent and hot-headed, Macmorris the stage Irishman reminds the audience of a level of militant resistance that is out of the ordinary. But the audience is also reminded that, as with all racism, what the colonial stereotype is suppressing closely resembles a part of us. What we deplore as innately inferior and negative in the Other – in this case the so-called belligerence of the Irish – is a projection of what we would much prefer not to acknowledge in ourselves: the violence of colonial rule.

What the character of Macmorris also shows, I think, is awareness that theatrical performance and social performance have something in common: they unsettle the fixity of an imposed identity. If only briefly, the scene with Macmorris makes us conscious of the damage that a stereotype can achieve, awakens our responsibility in relation to this damage and indicates that theatrical performance may also function as a means of exposing it. Shakespeare's use of the stage Irishman should not blind us, however, to the ways in which this figure may also be deployed to reinforce and to gloss over systems of inequality and injustice. The portrayal of the priest Foigard in Farquhar's popular eighteenth-century comedy *The Beaux' Stratagem* is a case in point.

Foigard is a minor character. He is a straightforward comic villain who makes a bungled attempt to smuggle the French count Bellair into the bedchamber of the virtuous and stalwartly English Mrs Sullen. Ineptly disguised as a French priest, Foigard is really a lecherous Roman Catholic Irishman. What gives Foigard away and renders his danger so relatively unthreatening is the irrepressibility of his brogue. Both the audience and the English hero of the play, Aimwell, can tell Foigard a mile away:

> AIMWELL: The son of a bogtrotter in Ireland.
> Sir, your tongue will condemn you before any
> bench in the kingdom.
>
> FOIGARD: And is your tongue all your evidensh,
> joy?
>
> AIMWELL: That's enough.
>
> FOIGARD: No, no, joy, for I vill never spake
> English no more.
>
> *(The Beaux' Stratagem*, 4.2.61–65)

Farquhar's depiction of a duplicitous Irish priest with incompetent English pronunciation forcing his way into the bedroom of a Protestant woman played to contemporary paranoia about untrustworthy and rapacious Irish Catholic rebels. As theatre historian Helen Burke points out in her 2003 study *Riotous Performances*, Foigard is presented as a cultural, religious and political deviant 'who needs the correction of British law' (p. 14). The stage Irishman in Farquhar's play thus feeds into the virulent anti-Catholic sectarianism of Irish Protestant sermons and histories of the early eighteenth century. To this extent, *The Beaux' Stratagem* shores up the extraordinary injustices of the Penal Laws, a series of legislative measures enacted by the Irish parliament from the 1690s that provided for the disarming of Catholics, the banning of Catholics from foreign seats of learning, the abolition of Catholic inheritance rights, the exclusion of Catholics from the professions and most aspects of public life, and the banishment of Catholic bishops and regular clergy. Although not all the Penal Laws were enforced and although many Irish Catholic gentry found imaginative ways to avoid some of their harsher restrictions, the overall effect was to make Irish Catholics into second-class citizens and to reduce by two-thirds the amount of land owned by Catholics. Farquhar's use of the stage Irishman shows that the Irish theatre in this period was closely connected to this wider political and sectarian context and that the theatre – then as now – was an instrument of political power.

But even here we must be wary of making an absolute pronouncement. If Foigard is condemned as a duplicitous actor, it is worth remembering that *The Beaux' Stratagem* is a play that celebrates disguise and the malleability of social identity. Its narrative tracks the romantic fortunes of the protagonist-hero, Aimwell, who is disguised as his titled brother, and of his friend Archer, who is disguised as Aimwell's servant. Much of the pleasure of the play derives from its portrayal of romantic success as far more a consequence of how you make things up as you go along than of who you are socially. In this context, Foigard's deviancy is not so much his pretending to be someone else but the recalcitrance of his accent. It is this that reveals what an early seventeenth-century audience would have seen as Foigard's instantly recognisable and unmovable Irishness. In a sea of disguises this is one identity that appears resolutely the same. Indeed, what complicates the political effect of this exceptionally popular play – produced in Dublin fifty-eight times between 1722 and 1758 – is that by the mid-eighteenth century, the idea of a stubborn, unerasable Irishness had acquired a great many positive associations for an Irish Protestant society that saw itself in dispute with England's political and economic interests. We shall be looking at the changing function of the Irish theatre in more detail in the next section, but for the moment my point is simply that although Foigard serves as an anti-Catholic and anti-Irish stereotype in Farquhar's play, his embodiment of a stolid Irishness also arouses countervailing emotions of admiration and respect. If there is anything that is fixed about theatre, you could say, it is that it isn't.

A sentimentalised version of the stage Irishman occurs in what is probably the best-known Irish nationalist melodrama, Boucicault's *The Shaughraun*. The play was performed in the 1870s with Boucicault in the title role, and in the context of Boucicault's much-publicised plea for clemency on behalf of Fenian Irish nationalist prisoners in England. The Fenians were a secret group of militant, separatist activists dedicated to the cause of Irish nationalism. In 1867, seven years before *The Shaughraun* was first performed, there was a botched Fenian prison escape attempt in Manchester that involved the shooting dead of a policeman and that aroused extensive anti-Irish feeling. Boucicault deals with this difficult historical event by altering and fictionalising it almost (but not quite) out of all recognition. Instead of working class and unemployed, the play's Fenian character is a young Irish aristocrat – Robert Ffolliott – swindled out of his inheritance by a scheming Catholic arriviste, Corry Kinchela. Conn, the character indicated by the play's title (which means 'landless peasant' or 'vagabond'), is presented as likeable, dextrous and eloquent, his overriding trait being fastidious loyalty to Robert, his aristocratic master. Any anxieties the audience might have regarding the Fenian physical-force tradition of separatist nationalism are resolved by a simple expedient: altering the facts. Fenians were not part of Ireland's largely pro-British hereditary aristocracy, nor was undying loyalty to the gentry a conspicuous characteristic of the nineteenth-century, post-Famine Irish peasant. In this regard, the characters in Boucicault's play translate the audience from hard reality to wishful thinking.

Sentimentalisation of this kind is especially evident in the play's concluding moments. Conn pleads with the audience to forgive him for his foibles (alcoholism, poaching and minor thievery) in the interests of a happy ending:

> CONN: You are the only friend I have. Long life t'ye! – Many a time have you looked over my faults – will you be blind to them now, and hould out your hands once more to a poor Shaughraun?
> OMNES: Hurroo! Hurroo! (*Till curtain*)
> (*The Shaughraun* [1987], p. 326)

'Hurroo! Hurroo!' is Boucicault's Irish version of the English cheer 'Hooray!' That all ('omnes') of the characters on stage shout out this applause is intended as a signal for the theatre audience to do likewise. By evoking our enjoyment of the play's performance, Boucicault encourages us to overlook not just Conn's misdemeanours but those of the entire Fenian enterprise. Importantly, it is our enjoyment of the play's narrative and our understanding of the workings of the institutional theatre that form the basis for this sleight of hand. Conn is not really Conn but an actor playing the part; in the 1870s this was Boucicault himself. If we can agree to be united by the fundamental convention of theatre – that an action is and is not at the same time – then, of course, the frightening drama of Fenian insurgency subsides. Instead of actions such as sporadic, seemingly random explosions, killings, maimings – acts that suggest a political logic at variance to our own – what we have in Boucicault's play is the familiar immediacy of entertainment. Maintaining an anti-Irish or even anti-Fenian feeling in this context is a mistake because it is so unnecessary. The spectator's benevolence may be short lived, but it arises because the play gives the impression that its way of looking at things is universal. Indeed, the Fenian challenge to British imperialism is made to seem so irrelevant that it can be rendered as a metaphor for its opposite: a romantic, comic endorsement of what we already know. To this extent, *The Shaughraun* in performance is imperialism in action.

Using the convention of the stage Irishman to proffer a solution to Anglo-Irish conflict along the lines of providing a theatre audience with whatever it finds least difficult to imagine is not so very different from seventeenth- and early eighteenth-century versions of the stage Irishman as a thick-headed boor. So well worn is the tactic of a stage Irishman playing up to the expectations of an English audience that it becomes one of Shaw's central ideas in his 1904 play *John Bull's Other Island*. With laborious Shavian pedantry, *John Bull's Other Island* suggests that Ireland and England are locked in a relationship that involves putting on performances for each other. Shaw's play implies that this condition has advanced so far that the essence of a romantic and sentimentalised Irishness is to be found in the solidly English character of Tom Broadbent, while English rationality and calculation emanate from the play's cool-headed Irishman, Larry Doyle. True to its Shavian wit, the play's stage Irishman, Tim Haffigan, is – of course – not Irish at all. Roman Catholic, garrulous (with an Irish accent) and alcoholic he is, certainly, but Haffigan, it turns out, is from Glasgow, Scotland. Shaw's mild complication of the stage Irishman and his idea that there exists nothing as tidy as a fixed national identity come at more or less the same time that, under the guidance of W. B. Yeats and Lady Gregory, Ireland's national theatre movement at the Abbey claimed it would reject the stage Irishman altogether. Given that *John Bull's Other Island* insists that the stage Irishman is a representation arising from a transactional process between England and Ireland and given Yeats and Gregory's opposing claim that the stage Irishman is simply a caricature to be rejected and that Irish theatre is exclusively national, it is not at all surprising that Shaw's play was not included in the national theatre's repertoire.

One way to consider the cultural role of the stage Irishman is as a calibration of the anxieties and interests of Britain's (and later Ireland's) political and economic elites. The stage Irishman is represented alternatively as loyal or belligerent, trustworthy or duplicitous, astute or ignorant, clever or cunning. Rebellions and threats of invasion in early eighteenth-century Ireland coincide with a stage Irishman who is dangerously irrational and zealously Roman Catholic; waves of Irish economic migration exploited for low-paid labour in Britain beginning in the mid-eighteenth century overlap with a sentimentalisation of Irish characters as loyal but clumsy; Fenian anti-colonial insurgency coincides with a stage Irishman who is loyal and entertaining and thus a perfect instrument to secure imperial hegemony.

In post-independence Ireland an obsession with religious and nationalist political rectitude and with the economic interests of a native Irish bourgeoisie resurrects the idea of the stage Irishman as working class and socially disruptive. Tom Murphy's brilliantly acerbic play *A Whistle in the Dark* confronts its audience with an Irish emigrant family in Coventry living out the stereotype of the violent Irish. So forceful is Murphy's achievement that the play was rejected by the Abbey Theatre on the grounds that no such people existed in Ireland, and it provoked the following comment from the London *Evening Standard*'s theatre critic Milton Shulman: 'The only thing that separates his characters from a bunch of wild gorillas is their ability to speak with an Irish accent. ... [The play] will probably set back Ireland's reputation for civilization at least 100 years' (quoted in Fintan

O'Toole, *The Politics of Magic*, 1987, p. 10). Yet the brilliance of Murphy's play lies in its suggestion that the stereotype of the violent Irish is a product not just of colonialism but also of the calcified class hierarchy of post-independence Irish society.

In each of the contexts in which he is deployed, what the stage Irishman attempts is to fix an identity. This fixing of identity is designed to secure the apparent certainty of a social, ethnic or political hierarchy. Specifically, the stage Irishman is a device that discredits Ireland's claim to political independence and the claim of its people to economic and political equality. Used historically as a way of lampooning the idea of the Irish Catholic peasant as a proper political subject and to justify military and economic repression, the stage Irishman is deployed today as a way of undermining the credibility of many of Ireland's marginalised social groups. Although it has its origins in colonialism, the device is not exclusively a product of colonialism. Indeed, as I suggested in my allusion to Murphy's *A Whistle in the Dark*, a version of the stage Irishman can serve the interests of a so-called postcolonial nationalism just as well. In his contemporary avatar, evident in the plays of Martin McDonagh, the stage Irishman mocks anyone unlucky enough to belong to the swelling ranks of the poor. And although politicians, bankers, land developers and the captains of big business are all noticeably absent from the narratives of McDonagh's plays, the use of the stage Irishman in a play such as *The Beauty Queen of Leenane* is just as brazenly political as anything from the late seventeenth or early eighteenth century at the time of the Penal Laws. With McDonagh, Ireland's current neo-colonial drive for foreign inward capital investment at all costs and the country's state-led rush to privatise health care and other social services coincide with a stage portrayal of recalcitrant rural communities populated with amoral dolts, foolish priests and psychotic celibates – in other words, a poor portrayed as *deserving* no support. The stage Irishman may have his origins in colonialism, but the figure is just as popular for bourgeois nationalism. It is a device that indicates a line of connection between the theatre as a colonial institution and the postcolonial institution of theatre in Ireland today.

Theatre history

From the earliest days of Irish theatre history writing until quite recently, the theatre in Ireland has been viewed as a cultural enterprise that begins in the early seventeenth century and that remains quite separate from earlier and contemporaneous indigenous performance traditions. Writing in the eighteenth century, Robert Hitchcock and Victor Turner viewed Ireland's city-based theatre as the exclusive site of theatrical performance: the place where theatrical performance was instituted as legitimate in the sense of according with London-based norms of representation. For them what had existed in Ireland before and alongside the arrival of institutional theatre was a puzzling absence. 'The peculiar exclusion of the stage appears all the more singular and extraordinary', writes Hitchcock in *An Historical View of the Irish Stage from the Earliest Period down to the Close of the*

Season 1788 (1794), 'as Ireland was so early celebrated as the seat of learning, and the parent of a succession of bards, poets, and men of eminent genius for several centuries' (p. 3). For Turner, in *The History of the Theatres of London and Dublin* (1761), the civilising and educational function of the theatre is its raison d'être, and he praised the reforming efforts of his contemporary Thomas Sheridan (the actor, playwright and owner of Dublin's Smock Alley Theatre) for 'raising the Irish theatre to an equal degree of respectability' (p. 155) in relation to its London counterparts. For Hitchcock and Turner this familiar, exciting, money-making, urban institution is the only form of theatre that can be imagined with the London theatre as the touchstone of aesthetic standards.

Owing in large part to the recent, groundbreaking scholarship of Alan J. Fletcher, we are now aware of a rich tradition of Gaelic performance in Ireland starting long before and continuing alongside the establishment of the institutional theatre in the early seventeenth century. Manuscript sources reveal that this tradition may date from as early as the eighth century and that it included a repertory of performers from professional poets, storytellers and satirists to performing artists and contortionists who specialised in wild and extravagant uses of the body, amounting to what Fletcher describes as 'a taxonomy of Gaelic performance the like of which is unequalled anywhere in the British Isles' (*Drama and the Performing Arts in Pre-Cromwellian Ireland*, 2001, p. 6). This performance tradition was highly physical and frequently involved complex interactions between performers and audience. A key figure was the *druth* (jester), whose performing skills might also have included juggling, gambolling, and acrobatics. Alongside singers, storytellers and mummers were *cruittiri* (harpers), *clessanaig* (jugglers, tricksters, acrobats) and *bragetori* (farters). In other words, when the formal institutional theatre so celebrated by Turner and Hitchcock begins in Ireland, it does so not in a vacuum but in the context of an existing, alternative and vibrantly physical theatrical tradition.

Nevertheless, as far as the institutional theatre is concerned, history begins with the social and political entrenchment of English settler colonialism in the early seventeenth century. Specifically, it commences with the establishment of Werburgh Street Theatre in Dublin (probably in 1635) on the orders of the English Lord Deputy, Thomas Wentworth, Earl of Strafford. Werburgh Street Theatre was run by John Ogilby, a Scottish dancing master who had been invited to Dublin by Wentworth to serve at the viceregal court as its master of revels. As the centre for English rule in Ireland, the city of Dublin was located in an area of secure settler colonial influence known as the 'Pale' – hence the danger implied in going anywhere 'beyond the Pale'. Werburgh Street Theatre itself was close to the headquarters of English administration at Dublin Castle. Ogilby's theatre was not a minor project: it featured a company of prestigious London actors and had the well-known English Catholic playwright James Shirley as its resident dramatist. A special box was built at the side of the stage to accommodate the Lord Deputy, and the first plays performed at the theatre – plays such as Shirley's *Saint Patrick for Ireland*

(1639) and Henry Burnell's *Landgartha* (1640) – expressed themes that strongly advocated on behalf of the English colonial mission in Ireland. Thus, to say that colonialism is a primary determinant of the theatre as an institution in Ireland is to make a statement that its founders would have thought so blindingly obvious as to be not worth saying at all. The Werburgh Street Theatre was an institution that existed, quite openly, as a vehicle for English vice-regal government and for the promotion of the values, prestige and sometimes divided loyalties of a settler colonial elite. As Christopher Morash's *A History of Irish Theatre 1601–2000* (2002) puts it, Werburgh Street Theatre brought together 'the tight circle of courts, castle and college that would form the foundation of Irish theatre audiences for almost two centuries' (p. 6). Except that it was in Dublin and catered to an audience living in Ireland, there was very little that was 'Irish' about Ireland's first theatre.

But this 'except' covers a big exception. Ironically, it is precisely the settler colonial function of the Werburgh Street Theatre (and of its 1662 successor, Smock Alley) that is responsible for transforming the Irish theatre's role from one of disparaging Ireland and glorifying colonialism to one of expressing and supporting an Irish identity. The theatre was an integral part of the social and cultural life of settler colonialism in Ireland, but this also meant that it became an important site for expressing the distinctiveness of that phenomenon. And what was most distinctive about it was that it was Irish. In other words, once the economic and political interests of settler colonialism in Ireland were at odds with those of the English political establishment – a process that, as in other sites of settler colonialism, was quite rapid – the theatre emerged as an institution that expressed a kind of nationalism, albeit a nationalism that was Protestant and often virulently anti-Roman Catholic. For example, from the end of the seventeenth century onwards, plays such as William Philips' *St Stephen's Green, or The Generous Lovers* (Smock Alley, Dublin, 1699), Thomas Sheridan's *The Brave Irishman* (Smock Alley, Dublin, 1743) and Charles Macklin's *Love à la Mode* (Drury Lane, London, 1759) sought to over-turn the negative connotations of the stage Irishman and to portray Ireland itself as unexpectedly refined. As we saw when we discussed the role of Foigard in *The Beaux' Stratagem*, even plays with anti-Catholic elements acquired a more complex political nuance when they were performed within this broader and rapidly changing cultural context.

Helen Burke's fascinating study of eighteenth-century Irish theatre, *Riotous Performances*, tracks these ambiguities and complexities in some detail. She shows, for example, how the 1712 performance at Dublin's Smock Alley Theatre of Nicholas Rowe's *Tamerlane*, a play that celebrates a Protestant Williamite victory over Catholicism and shores up the idea that there should be punitive laws against Catholics, *also* manages to articulate a frustrated Irish Protestant and settler colonial desire for constitutional and economic parity with England (p. 51). Burke's point is that even if *Tamerlane* was anti-Catholic in sentiment, its insistence on freedom and lib-erty from the tyranny of an autocratic British administration held suggestive and politically productive meanings for Irish

Catholics as well as Irish Protestants. In a similar fashion, Jonathan Swift's project to encourage the wearing of Irish-made and Irish-styled costumes in the theatre in the 1720s and 1730s demonstrated settler colonial annoyance at the prevailing trade laws between Britain and Ireland in a manner that *also* gestured to an imagined national community beyond the English Pale. By the end of the eighteenth century, such nationalist or proto-nationalist tendencies had become more explicit. Dramatist and actor John O'Keeffe toured Ireland with plays that included nationalist songs and references to local places and people – plays such as O'Keeffe's own immensely popular *The Wicklow Mountains* (Covent Garden, London, 1798). We know too that from the 1770s the actor Robert Owenson interspersed his performances with Irish music and Irish-language phrases. This nationalistic trend in late eighteenth-century Irish theatre culminated in December 1784 when Owenson set up a short-lived 'national theatre' in Dublin. According to his daughter, the novelist Lady Morgan, Owenson believed that theatres should be erected 'like Martello towers, at regular intervals over the land for the protection and instruction of the national mind' (quoted in Burke, *Riotous Performances*, p. 285).

Many of these developments reflected the changing nature of the population of eighteenth-century Dublin and thus of its theatre audiences. By the closing decades of the 1700s Dublin had transformed from a city with a Protestant majority in the early part of the century to one that was predominantly Roman Catholic. Many of the Catholics and Protestants who attended the theatre came from Dublin's rural hinterland and were deeply familiar with the performance traditions and theatrical practices of Gaelic Ireland. This may be one reason why audiences at the Dublin theatres during this period were so notoriously outspoken: spectators shouted out and clapped or booed not only the actors on stage but the arrival in the theatre of visiting notables. So noisy were these vociferations that on one occasion in 1784 the English Viceroy filled the upper gallery of the pro-government Theatre Royal at Smock Alley with soldiers, servants and a rented crowd to forestall the possibility of large-scale booing (Burke, *Riotous Performances*, pp. 274–75). On another occasion a hostile crowd pursued the Lord Deputy from the theatre to the gates of Dublin Castle. The degree to which the theatre in Ireland had become a site of resistance to the British state – what Burke describes as a place of 'riotous performances' – is further demonstrated by the Irish parliament's introduction of a Stage Act in 1786. This legislation insisted that all theatrical activity in Ireland be controlled by government licence. By making the theatre dependent on government patronage, the Stage Act was designed to restrict the ways in which the theatre in Ireland had become a site of political resistance and nationalist activity. It sought to achieve this by establishing the theatre's dependency on the state; to this day, this close and (I believe) damagingly uncritical relationship to the state remains one of the Irish theatre's most problematic features.

The Stage Act of 1786 served as an impediment but did not by any means arrest the operation of theatre in Ireland as an important site for generating political protest and as a means of composing new ways of thinking about politics. It is true that throughout the nineteenth century and into the early twentieth century, the vice-regal box remained the most prized seat in the theatre and that the epithet 'royal' continued to be regarded by many as just as unambiguously prestigious as the term 'national'. Visits by the Lord Lieutenant (before the Act of Union in 1801, the Lord Deputy) to the theatre in the nineteenth century were still regular and grand occasions. Even in the case of the Irish Literary Theatre, which was set up in 1897 as a nationalist response to colonial misrepresentations of Ireland, the amended subclause under which the theatre was established – a subsection of the Local Government Act – underlined the criticality to theatre of British state authority in Ireland (Pilkington, *Theatre and the State in Twentieth-Century Ireland*, 2001, p. 7).

Despite these restrictions, during the century that followed the 1790s the theatres of Belfast and Dublin functioned as extraordinarily free social spaces that were shared by all social classes and by Catholics and Protestants alike. This bestowed on the theatre an air of intense political excitement – one that brought together a freedom from ordinary constraints and a performative atmosphere that encouraged putting on a role, acting up and acting differently. Acting up by means of protests was a regular feature of theatre attendance. In Dublin, during the opening decades of the nineteenth century, for example, Orangemen (zealously Protestant unionists who supported the retention of Ireland's political union with England) used the theatre space to demonstrate their displeasure with the British government's increasingly conciliatory moves towards Irish Catholics, and Irish nationalists used theatre performances to campaign for Catholic emancipation and home rule. There were shouts, groans, cheers, chanting and singing. Performances of plays with national themes – Boucicault's melodramas, for instance – tended especially to provoke dramatic responses from the audience. In his 2007 essay 'Modernity, Geography and Historiography', Mark Phelan notes that in 1819 Belfast's Grand Opera House installed a giant stage net to catch steel rivets ('Belfast confetti') thrown at the stage, and he observes that these ructions inside the theatre were not matched by disturbances outside. Phelan's point is that this suggests the theatre was a site that encouraged strong – sometimes violent – displays of political feeling in a manner that was itself theatrical and performative and that was set off from the world outside the theatre (pp. 142–44).

Despite the strikingly histrionic character of theatre protests, the discipline of theatre history tends to render the performance of protests as a phenomenon that is wholly illegitimate. The word 'riot' as a descriptor of theatre protests – as in *The Playboy of the Western World* (Abbey Theatre, Dublin, 1907) 'riots' or the 'riots' associated with the first performance of O'Casey's *The Plough and the Stars* (Abbey Theatre, Dublin, 1926) – suggests unreasonableness, illegitimacy and a lack of control. Whereas the word 'protest' implies a point of view, the word 'riot' denotes violence. But this partisan use of language results in a skewed view of theatre and its effect on audiences. Whether they involve shouting out, groaning or physically climbing on stage and making a speech, protests in the theatre are performances that insist theatre is something more than an ordered enactment of a play. 'The public sphere reconfigured in the echoing space of extravagant action' is how Nicholas Allen assesses the importance of theatrical and other protests in 1920s Dublin in *Modernism, Ireland and Civil War* (2009, p. 42). Theatre, such actions declare, is a collective experience, and enacting a protest as well as acting a play tests and stretches our conceptions of ordinary action in a way that is experimental and revelatory.

When audience members sang 'A Nation Once Again' during the 1907 protests against Synge's *The Playboy of the Western World*, what they were asserting was not just their objection to Synge's comedy but the relevance and vitality of a counter-culture that was oral, affective and energetically participative. Likewise, when a group of Derry actors protesting against Vincent Woods' *At the Black Pig's Dyke* (Druid Lane Theatre, Galway, 1992) walked on to the stage at the end of the play and performed a final unscripted scene that drew attention to the play's pro-British government politics, it was not just a political point that was being made; the protestors were drawing deliberate attention to a counter-culture of anti-colonial activism based in part on the radical dramaturgy of the Brazilian director Augusto Boal and in part on the interventions of republican activism. Protesting in the theatre is about insisting that the world is open to change and that the act of acting up is itself a contribution to that change.

For many critics and commentators the point at which Irish theatre begins is quite exact: 8 May 1899, the date of the first production of the Irish Literary Theatre. This view of the national literary theatre movement of the late nineteenth century and early twentieth century as Ireland's first authentic national theatre institution emanates from the writings of its founders, chiefly Lady Augusta Gregory and W. B. Yeats. For Yeats and Gregory the setting up of the Irish Literary Theatre as a national literary institution was nothing less than a cultural watershed. As with most foundational announcements, their statement is wildly exaggerated. Even the inaugural production of the Irish Literary Theatre – Yeats' *The Countess Cathleen* – followed a première of the play in January 1899 at the English Chief Secretary's lodge at the Phoenix Park in Dublin. Moreover, the combination of Irish material with a positive, anti-colonial representation of Ireland was by no means unique to the Irish Literary Theatre or its successors. It was also a crucial and conspicuous feature of Boucicault's Irish melodramas and of the virtual subgenre of nationalist melodrama that was performed with regularity from the late 1880s up until the 1920s at the Queen's Royal Theatre. For Yeats and Gregory these previous nationalist initiatives were, by turns, unidealistic, inauthentic or simply invisible. In *Our Irish Theatre*,

Gregory quotes from a letter circulated to the theatre's potential guarantors:

> We propose to have performed in Dublin in the
> spring of every year certain Celtic and Irish plays,
> which whatever be their degree of excellence will
> be written with a high ambition, and so to build
> up a Celtic and Irish school of dramatic litera-
> ture. We hope to find in Ireland an uncorrupted
> and imaginative audience trained to listen by its
> passion for oratory, and believe that our desire
> to bring upon the stage the deeper thoughts and
> emotions of Ireland will ensure for us a tolerant
> welcome, and that freedom to experiment which
> is not found in theatres of England, and without
> which no new movement in art or literature can
> succeed. We will show that Ireland is not the
> home of buffoonery and of easy sentiment, as it
> has been represented, but the home of an ancient
> idealism. We are confident of the support of all
> Irish people, who are weary of misrepresenta-
> tion, in carrying out a work that is outside all the
> political questions that divide us. (p. 20)

Gregory's purpose is to establish a contrast between, on the one hand, the inauthentic representations of Ireland that had existed before the Irish Literary Theatre initiative and, on the other, the far more authentic representations of Ireland that the Irish Literary Theatre promised to nourish and promote. Important points in the declaration are that the theatre would draw upon and express an older oral tradition (Ireland's 'passion for oratory') and that in rendering positive representations of Ireland it would bring people together in a way that would transcend politics: 'outside all the political questions that divide us'. Implicit in Yeats and Gregory's idealistic statement is not only the idea of the theatre as a unifying nationalist force but an idea of theatre as a cultural practice that refines and develops older (and by implication less sophisticated) cultural traditions such as storytelling, balladry and political oratory. This theatre outside the theatre is what I would now like briefly to consider.

Theatre outside the theatre 1

> I have now seen the great English actors, and heard plays in the English tongue, but poor and dull they seemed to me after the acting of our own people at the wakes and fairs; for it is a truth, the English cannot make us weep and laugh as I have seen the crowds with us when the players played and the poets recited their songs. (Quoted in Fletcher, *Drama, Performance and Polity*, p. 43)

This anonymous remark is recorded by Speranza Wilde (Oscar's mother) as having been made in the late 1880s and is a testament to the endurance of alternative theatre and performance traditions in Ireland during the nineteenth century. Studies by folklore scholars Alan Gailey, Gearóid Ó Crualaoich and Henry Glassie show that a variety of theatrical and quasi-theatrical performances took place in the Irish countryside, mostly in the eighteenth and nineteenth centuries. These performances – of patterns, mumming as well as the ceremonies of strawboys and wren boys – continued into the twentieth century and occurred mainly at wakes, weddings and fairs and on seasonal dates in the rural calendar such as Halloween or *samhain*, Christmas, and at the start of summer or *bealtaine*. Some of these traditions have continued, at least vestigially, until the present: on St Stephen's Day (26 December), for example, one can still find wren boys – groups of young men or sometimes children costumed outlandishly in skirts and dresses who travel from house to house performing a song about the capture of the wren. There isn't enough space in this book to describe all these practices, or indeed to elaborate on any one of them in detail, so what follow are necessarily brief accounts.

From the seventeenth to the early twentieth century, mumming took place mainly at Christmastime, during the period from the mid-winter solstice to the early new year, and tended to involve groups of between eight and fourteen young men (Gailey, *Irish Folk Drama*, 1969, p. 14) dressed in straw costumes and conical helmets and led by a captain. The mummers concealed their identities from their prospective audiences – so when they turned up at the door of a house and the captain shouted out, 'Any admittance for the mummers?', the resident might well think twice before she replied. These young men could be your good friends, your neighbours or your relatives, or they could be notorious troublemakers. Unlike the institutional theatre, mumming begins not with brandishing a paid-for ticket at an usher but with making an invitation of hospitality in exchange for entertainment. To that extent, one's response to the captain of the mummers was a response delivered not just to them but also through them to the community as a whole.

The words 'come in' provide the crucial signal that a performance of mumming is about to begin. The practice of mumming is fundamentally different from the working of a performance in the institutional theatre. In the case of the latter we know the identity of the actor, and for the duration of the performance we simply imagine that the actor on stage *is* the character that she or he is playing. Imagining that Dion Boucicault is Conn in *The Shaughraun*, for example, is a metaphorical process. We know that Boucicault is not Conn, but we accept that he is acting the part of this character for the duration of the play's performance.

When mummers entered a house the performance began with music and a dance. After this came a drama whose characters and narrative followed a well-known formula. There was a hero-protagonist (often called Saint Patrick or Sir Sopin), a villain (who might be called Prince George or Oliver Cromwell), a mad doctor with a collection of insanely inadequate medical accoutrements and sometimes a devil with a frying pan on his shoulder. The narrative theme was impossible revival. Clouted over the head with a Cromwellian sword, Saint Patrick would collapse to the ground, apparently dead. During a long, boastful speech by Cromwell and a fantastic series of surgical manoeuvres by the doctor, Saint Patrick would be revived and would then take his final, successful and fatal revenge: the grand comeuppance of Mr Cromwell. Performances ended with a dance between the mummers and some or all of the people in whose house they had just performed. If money was collected, it was collected for a mummers' ball or for a Christmas dance attended by all who had contributed or for a local charity (Gailey, *Irish Folk Drama*, pp. 12–13).

Another crucial element of mummers' plays was the way in which the rhymes that were recited tended to include references to the locality of the performance, to individual members of the audience, to recent events in the area or to the precise and immediate circumstances of performance. Again, it is illuminating to contrast this with the methods of the institutional theatre, where performances strive to repeat themselves as exactly as possible and as a result are conspicuously *without* any reference to the immediate local circumstance, history or context of performance.

What I have been suggesting is that there are important distinctions of cultural value between the way in which the institutional theatre works and the way in which traditions such as mumming work. In most cases, the institutional theatre functions as a business – an urban and primarily money-making venture – and affirms a universal aesthetic experience. For mumming, as for other impromptu rural performances, the social and cultural priority of the exercise is social disruption and the revival and reproduction of a community. The disruptions performed by the mummers complemented their narratives of impossible revival; what was at issue in both was the idea of the primacy of the community over the interests, preoccupations and, sometimes, desires of the individual.

In addition to being an extensively practised funeral rite and social occasion, the Irish wake was an important site for non-institutional theatrical performance. With the corpse of the deceased still in the house, the family in mourning offered hospitality to sympathising neighbours, relatives and friends. Sympathisers often stayed awake for long hours praying alongside the dead body and remembering and celebrating the life of the deceased. With their mixture of traumatic grief, exhaustion, storytelling, music, reminiscence and substantial quantities of alcohol, wakes held the potential for unusually rambunctious behaviour. Until the mid-twentieth century in some areas, there were also specific games or performances that enlivened the boisterous atmosphere of what was known as the 'merry wake'. The following description was written in 1852 by the County Kilkenny antiquarian John Prim:

> These wake games are never performed in the houses of persons who felt really afflicted by the bereavement which they might be supposed to have endured in the demise of a member of their family. They are reserved for the deaths of old people who had survived the ordinary span of life, or young children who cannot be looked upon as an irreparable loss. They are placed

under the conduct of some peasant of the dis-
trict who excelled in rustic wit and humour, and
this person, under the title of 'borekeen', may be
termed the hierophant of the observances, whose
orders are carried into force by subordinate
officers, all arrayed in fantastic habilments. ... The
game called 'Hold the light', in which a man is
blindfolded and flogged, has been looked upon
as a profane travestie [*sic*] of the passion of our
Lord; and religion might also be considered as
brought into contempt by another of the series,
in which a person caricaturing a priest and wearing a rosary composed of small potatoes strung
together, enters into conflict with the 'borekeen'
and is put down and expelled from the room by
direction of the latter. (Quoted in Ó Crualaoich,
'The "Merry Wake"', 1998, p. 193)

Commenting on this description, Ó Crualaoich remarks that
performance games functioned both as forms of resistance
and as forms of social solidarity and continuity. Like the
great wheeling routines that preceded nineteenth-century
faction fights and that involved routine gymnastic moves,
chants, stylized gestures and insults, practices such as 'Hold
the light' were performances that conveyed an exuberant
sense of personal endurance and defiance.

What is worthy of note in these cases is that the actor
is viewed not as the spectator's imaginary delegate (which
is the view that prevails in the institutional theatre) but as

performing a role that is felt to be interchangeable with that of a spectator and that, crucially, involves real as well as imaginary actions. Interestingly, the theatrical and exhibitionist elements of such performance tended to be viewed in the early twentieth century as an embarrassing anomaly, as in a Gaelic League description of the noisy acoustics of *sean-nós* (old-style) Irish dancing as 'un-Irish' and 'too acrobatic' (see Helen Brennan, *The Story of Irish Dance*, 1999, pp. 40–41). Highly important to the symbolic life of Ireland's rural non-elite, these forms of performance tend to be recorded in the literary and cultural revival of the period under the anodyne category of 'the folk'. From theatre histories they are all but absent. Nevertheless, these practices are critical to a more inclusive cultural history because they tell us something important about the ways in which Irish culture conceived of social action itself.

Violence

Violence is often associated with thinking about Ireland. As we have seen, Irishness has been characterised as inherently belligerent, and Ireland has been the site for extraordinary acts of brutal colonial repression as well as acts of violent rebellion and terrorist and anti-colonial defiance. With the anti-colonial military actions of the 1916 Easter Rising and the IRA's guerrilla war against British rule during the period 1919–21, violent actions underpin the Irish state, as they do all states. Nevertheless, violence, bloody violence, is something that unites us in abhorrence. It is also something that we tend to think of as providing a crucial measure of a bad politics. A person who incites or supports violence is not a good citizen. Many governments now argue that such people should be locked up, deported or, at the very least, made subject to strict censorship and to an all-encompassing surveillance. There are even governments that turn a blind eye to the inflicting of excruciating pain on such people (www.amnesty.org/en/counter-terror-with-justice). How we think about violence is closely linked to how we think about political change. And yet violence in relation to theatrical culture specifically is a conjunction that is not often considered.

The association of violence with certain kinds of performance and cultural practice is what I want to explore in this section. Through an analysis of J. M. Synge's *The Playboy of the Western World* (Abbey Theatre, Dublin, 1907) I want to argue that violence is used as a stigma to denigrate an alternative tradition of performance in Irish culture and so delegitimise the possibility of a radically alternative way of thinking about culture and about politics. I have chosen *The Playboy of the Western World* because it is a landmark play in Irish theatre history. Not only did it provoke substantial nationalist objection when it was first performed in January 1907 (the famous *Playboy* 'riots'), but in resisting nationalist protest Synge's play soon secured a reputation as a *cause célèbre* for the literary and artistic credentials of the Abbey Theatre. In Lady Gregory's *Our Irish Theatre*, 'The Fight Over the *Playboy*' is presented as a vital event in the development of a prestigious national theatre institution.

Synge's play is set in a *shebeen* (or country public house) 'on a wild coast of Mayo' in the rural west of Ireland. Talk about violence dominates the play's opening scene, in which Pegeen prepares for her wedding to the timorous Shawn Keogh by lamenting the loss from the locality of the physically more rambunctious and heroic men of the past: 'Where now will you meet the like of Daneen Sullivan knocked the eye from a peeler, or Marcus Quin, God rest him, got six months for maiming ewes' (pp. 69–70). Later in this scene, when the newly arrived Christy Mahon reveals that he killed his father with the blow of a *loy* (a narrow-bladed spade used for cutting turf), the news begins Christy's elevation as the community's attractive centre of attention. So impressed is Pegeen's father that he immediately invites Christy to spend the night in his house, as 'potboy' and protector to Pegeen. The more violence is involved in the narration of Christy's story, the more fascinated and delighted are his audience. In Act 2, with the arrival of three young women longing 'to set eyes ... on a man killed his father' (p. 83), bloody actions carry an almost sexual allure. The people of the play's County Mayo setting thrive on celebrations of outlandish physical violence.

Synge's preoccupation with the strangely positive attitudes of an Irish rural community towards violence is evident from an early stage in the play's composition. In the earliest one-page outline, entitled 'The Murderer: A Farce', a man who admits to killing his father is immediately elected as a county councillor. Despite the fact that all available statistics for the period suggest that Irish society was relatively peaceful, Synge's play draws on a perceived association between violence and the Irish peasant. It was an association that evoked widely held contemporary metropolitan interest mainly because of the use of physical force and intimidation in the Land War waged by tenants and clandestine rural insurgency groups against landlords in the 1880s. Irrespective of political allegiance, for a theatre audience that saw itself as modern, sophisticated and cosmopolitan, violent action was a thing of fascination and worry. For nationalists, for whom a tradition of anti-colonial insurrection was a core feature of their ideological inheritance, the idea that rural Irish society should be viewed as glamorising such acts carried connotations of an intrinsic Irish political volatility. In confirming contemporary stereotypes of the 'feckless Irish', rural Ireland's alleged volatile belligerence threatened the nationalist parliamentary campaign for home rule. For Irish unionists – those who favoured maintaining the 1801 Act of Union between Ireland and England – and particularly for those southern Irish unionists aware of the likely imminence of some form of home rule, the notion of an Irish peasant toleration of violence evoked the terrors of the Land War and stimulated concerns about the prospect of majority rule. Mention of animal maiming also served as a reminder that such acts still occurred in disputes between tenants and landlords and had been a feature of the conflict between graziers and peasants in the early 1900s. However framed, violence suggests an inassimilable difference.

In Synge's play Christy's story about killing his father 'with the blow of a loy' is told with such narrative panache and extravagant embellishment that Christy is soon regarded as a hero by the community, and this in turn causes him to transform himself into an all-powerful heroic figure. By the beginning of Act 3, Christy is described as a champion sportsman and a gamester: 'bringing bankrupt ruin on the roulette man, and the trick-o-the-loop man, and breaking the nose of the cockshot man, and winning all in the sports below, racing, lepping, dancing, and the Lord knows what!' (p. 96). But when it emerges that Christy's father, Old Mahon, is not dead, as Christy had both claimed and believed, Christy's attractiveness disappears. It disappears for Pegeen, who had fallen in love with him, and for the rural County Mayo community of which she is a member. Now describing Christy as a 'liar and the fool of men' (p. 107), Pegeen and the on-stage 'Crowd' accuse him of being an impostor. Christy responds by offering to kill his father 'again', in the belief that in doing so he will recover his reputation as a champion and Pegeen's love in earnest. Pegeen's reaction, however, is an even stronger repudiation.

> CHRISTY: ... [*To Pegeen*.] And what is it you'll say to me and I after doing it this time in the face of all?
> PEGEEN: I'll say, a strange man is a marvel with his mighty talk; but what's a squabble in your back-yard, and the blow of a loy, have taught me

that there's a great gap between a gallous story
and a dirty deed. [*To Men*] Take him on from
this, or the lot of us will be likely put on trial for
his deed to-day.

(p. 110)

From this point on, the response of the local community,
including Pegeen, is unanimous: they reject outright the
person they had previously considered a hero. The local men
attempt to tie Christy with a rope and drag him from the
house, and, with this abrupt change, Pegeen now attacks
him by burning his leg with a sod of turf (p. 111).

What produces this adverse change in the community's
attitude towards Christy is not so much the people's realisation that Christy's story is a fabrication as their awareness
that it has been exposed as a fabrication: it is now nothing
more than a fiction, and Christy, therefore, is a liar. This is
construed by Synge as a form of cowardice. The local people
do not object to violence when it is part of a narrative which
they can think of as real, but they recoil altogether when it
is committed directly in front of them or when it is revealed
to them to be wholly fictional.

Pegeen's lament, 'there's a great gap between a gallous
story and a dirty deed' (p. 110), encapsulates the dramatist's point. This rural County Mayo community seems to
regenerate itself through narratives of violence that glam-
orise brutal local crimes. But the actuality of retributive
violence with which the community is threatened when
Christy offers to kill his father 'again' belongs to a wholly

different category of experience. Synge's final perception is that the strength and maturity of the individual are directly proportionate to the individual's resistance to the will of the community. Christy comes to maturity not only by asserting authority over his father but by condemning the locality as perceptually impoverished. At the moment when rural west of Ireland society is revealed as craven, priest-fearing and hypocritical, Christy emerges as a fully integrated individual.

The play ends with Christy's triumphant rejection of the Mayo community and his re-energised sense of personal achievement: 'Ten thousand blessings upon all that's here, for you've turned me a likely gaffer in the end of all, the way I'll go romancing through a romping lifetime from this hour to the dawning of the judgment day' (p. 111). Pegeen, in contrast, covers her head with a shawl and, subsiding into the anonymous world of the traditional, utters a sound like keening – in the words of the stage directions, *'breaking out into wild lamentations'* (p. 112). Pegeen has changed from individual to generic peasant. For the theatre audience, what takes place in the closing moments of *The Playboy of the Western World* is also a form of superior self-realisation. What Pegeen cannot conceive of – that crucially important 'suspension of disbelief' in which things are and are not at the same time – is the precondition for our experience in the theatre. What for Pegeen is a tragic and disillusioning revelation – 'there's a great gap between a gallous story and a dirty deed' – is for the theatre audience merely an axiom, a basic precondition for theatrical acting and of its existence as an audience. Instead of looking at Christy as an actor, which is how we in the audience consider him, Pegeen views him as a liar. To this important extent, Christy and the theatre audience are separated from Pegeen and the Mayo community by an unbridgeable epistemological gulf. What and how we know is very different from what and how this peasant community is able to know. It is a gulf between the modernity of our world – the world of the theatre audience – and the traditional world of the represented Mayo.

What Pegeen laments at the end of the play, therefore, is not at all the same thing she mourned at its beginning. In Act 1, what Pegeen lamented when she evoked the memory of the storyteller and animal maimer Marcus Quin was a particular kind of political and cultural élan: 'and he a great warrant to tell stories of holy Ireland till he'd have the old women shedding down tears about their feet' (p. 70). Here the affectivity of Marcus Quin's storytelling is associated with the violent methods of fugitive agrarian insurgency groups such as the Whiteboys or the contemporary intimidatory methods of the United Irish League. In contrast, what Pegeen laments at the end of the play is her exclusion from a world of romantic love. She is excluded because she has excluded herself. Pegeen, and the Mayo community of which she is a part, are presented as unable to grasp a fundamental assumption of theatrical illusion: that the dramatic action that takes place is both true and not true, and that the actor on stage both is and is not the character that she is playing.

But is it possible to describe the aesthetic principle that informs Pegeen's rejection of Christy in a manner that is not pejorative? Could it be that what is rejected by Pegeen is not the theatrical imagination as such but a particular way of thinking about the imagination, and that the perceptual basis for this rejection has an equal validity? For Synge's peasant community, the transforming power of the imagination has to be based on a foundational incident regarded as fact. Take away this fact, or expose the foundational incident as a lie, and this transforming power collapses utterly – hence Pegeen's belief that once it has become obvious that Christy has not killed his father, his status changes irrevocably from playboy-hero to impostor and sham.

The cultural practices associated with the Mayo community in *The Playboy of the Western World* – Marcus Quin's storytelling; the drunken post-wake ballad singing of Pegeen's father, Michael James; fairground games such as the 'trick of the loop man' and 'cockshot man'; Christy's 'racing, lepping, dancing, and the Lord knows what' – are based not on the idea of the actor as the audience's imaginative delegate but on the idea of the actor or performer as a skilful champion. This is a conception of acting much closer to the Gaelic concept of the *druth* than to any immediately recognisable concept from the modern theatre. Its performance conveys an exuberant sense of personal endurance and defiance. As in the story of Daneen Sullivan, 'who knocked the eye from the peeler', the actor is viewed as an achiever of extraordinary physical feats whose memory is kept alive through a network of performative actions from balladry to storytelling. Compared with the acting that characterises the modern urban institutional theatre, which does not physically alter or affect objects, the acting of Synge's rural Mayo community has a more complex function. It takes place in conjunction with community-based events such as the wake and the gathering of neighbours or on the periphery of rural Ireland's largest commercial and social event, the fair. Most importantly, it marks the existence of a resilient but increasingly residual and largely unrecorded non-elite peasant culture. The imaginative and recreational practices of this rural non-elite do include a form of performative acting that is characterised by what institutional theatre thinks of as a willing suspension of disbelief, but not – as in the case of Christy's account of having killed his father – if the foundational incident of such acting is exposed as transparently fictional.

In other words, rather than simply functioning as entertainment, the performative acting depicted by Synge in his Mayo peasant community operates mnemonically: it exists as a historical testament to the power of the community to survive despite the odds. For performances to be valued by the peasant community, they must have *both* these functions: that of memory and that of transformation. In Synge's play, however, this cultural tradition is presented not just as inextricably associated with violence but also as perceptually inept. Rather like Yeats' use of the word 'riot' to describe the nationalist protests against *The Playboy of the Western World*, this distancing of peasant performances obstructs us from considering them of equal value to the cultural tradition of the institutional theatre. And for criticism to accept such a hierarchy today is damaging to the cultural knowledge that theatre and performance provide.

Acting natural and acting national

One reason for the enduring international popularity of Irish theatre is the range of cultural and political reassurances it offers, presenting its audiences with actions that are distinctly Irish and also recognisably natural. With the notable exception of the plays of Samuel Beckett, which provide a radical critique of naturalism and nationality, Irish drama presents sequences of action that are instantly familiar. An Irish play may be shocking, startling and thematically subversive, but the action that it presents on stage is most likely to be a version of behaviours that we know to be true. It was this axiomatic knotting together of nationalism and naturalism that so incensed Beckett and that accounts in part for his diatribe against the very idea of an Irishness expressed in art. Writing to his friend Thomas McGreevy on 31 January 1938, Beckett complained of his 'chronic inability to understand as member of any proposition a phrase like "the Irish people", or to imagine that it ever gave a fart in its corduroys for any form of art whatsoever' (*The Letters of Samuel Beckett 1920–1940*, 2009, p. 599). Beckett's view that nationalist art amounts to a contradiction is also evident in his astringent and resolutely anti-naturalistic dramaturgy and in the way in which his plays refuse any national attribution. Instead of the dustbins of Beckett's *Endgame* (Royal Court Theatre, London, 1957), the anonymous 'country road' of *Waiting*

for Godot (Théâtre de Babylon, Paris, 1953) or the illuminated mouth in *Not I* (Lincoln Center, New York, 1972),
conjure up the action of a drama by Synge, O'Casey, Friel,
Murphy, Carr, McDonagh or Enda Walsh. Despite many
differences among their works, what the latter dramatists
present are forms of action and behaviour that are immediately recognisable.

The tenacity of naturalism in Irish drama is rooted in
the importance given by a dominant national theatre tradition to the task of demonstrating an Irishness that can
be easily recognised and in the idea that Ireland must be
released into modernity. One valuable effect of the naturalistic style of acting championed in the 1900s by the Fay
brothers, Frank and William, and for which the early
Abbey Theatre became so famous, was its presentation of
Irish actions and forms of behaviour as decorously familiar. If we think of performance along the lines of Richard
Schechner's idea of 'restored behaviour' ('Restoration of
Behavior', 1981), what took place on the stage of Ireland's
national theatre institution in the early twentieth century
was a performance that showed Irish bodies moving in recognisably modern ways. In striking contrast, for example,
to the weird gesticulations of a ululating funeral keener,
the straw-masked performances of a mummer or the gro-
tesque and often crudely sexual and violent indecorousness
of a wake game, acting in the institutional theatre rendered
behaviour that was reassuringly and instantly recognisable
as modern. Modern but not modernist, this dominant naturalistic style of acting at the Abbey Theatre contrasts with

the deliberately disconcerting and provocative experiments of Beckett and, briefly, with the more expressionistic and provocative forms of theatre at Dublin's Gate Theatre in the 1920s and 1930s and with some productions for the Pike Theatre Club in the 1950s. For Ireland's social and political elites keen to distance themselves from all forms of revolutionary and anti-colonial militancy, sporadic violence and peasant insurrection, the naturalistic tendency of Irish theatre offered a perfect mechanism through which this distance could be achieved.

If naturalism is the signature tune of Irish theatre, then, this is because acting natural has many attractions for a country eager to claim a postcolonial national independence. It offers the reassurance that national identity can be realised through forms of behaviour that seem normal and that show action itself as constrained by known and familiar conventions. In a country where traditions of militant republican insurgency are never so very far away, naturalism's insistence that actions follow logically from explicable motives has a politically reassuring effect. During the literary revival of the late 1890s and early 1900s, this reassurance works in support of a thematic preoccupation with an unequivocal abandonment of non-constitutional forms of political agency. Broadly speaking, the Irish theatre movement of this period was more a project of recuperation than one of radical change. Along with the nationalist melodramas of Boucicault, Hubert O'Grady and J. W. Whitbread, the plays of the Irish Literary Theatre (and, from 1904, the Abbey) portrayed the traditional sites and themes of popular insurgency and political tension in Ireland (such as landlord/ tenant conflict, the 1798 rebellion, and famine) as consistent with a contemporary scheme of national modernisation. In all cases, political action was shown as motivated by a heightened sense of individual conscience and directed towards some form of constitutional autonomy. Plays such as Whitbread's *Lord Edward, or '98* (Queen's Theatre, Dublin, 1894), Yeats' *Cathleen Ni Houlihan* (Saint Teresa's Hall, Dublin, 1902) and Lady Gregory's *The Rising of the Moon* (Abbey Theatre, Dublin, 1907) portray insurgency exclusively in terms of individual volition. In much the same way, the notion of a national drama itself sought to replace what were regarded as premodern cultural forms (such as wakes, mumming and other 'folk' practices) with theatre, a cultural practice fully consistent with the idea of the state as a community of individual subjects or citizens. This was even more the case for the newly independent Irish state of the 1920s; for the state, the ideological benefit of O'Casey's *The Shadow of a Gunman* (Abbey Theatre, Dublin, 1923), *Juno and the Paycock* (Abbey Theatre, Dublin, 1924) and *The Plough and the Stars* (Abbey Theatre, Dublin, 1926) was that these plays interpreted acts of insurgency in terms of a misunderstanding of the fundamental conventions of theatre. In characters such as Minnie Powell in *Shadow*, Mary Boyle and Captain Boyle in *Juno* or Jack Clitheroe, The Covey or Uncle Peter in *The Plough*, believing in political militancy is shown to be a kind of theatrical cluelessness.

It is not so surprising, therefore, that around the time of Ireland's political independence (1922) theatre was often evoked as a way of distinguishing good politics from bad. One of the best and most revealing illustrations of this tendency is Yeats' story about a protestor at the first performance of *The Plough and the Stars*. Yeats relates how a young republican/nationalist, objecting to the way in which O'Casey's play attacks the motivation of the executed leaders of the 1916 Easter Rising, climbed on stage and, while standing there, noticed an actress frozen in the posture of the part that she had been playing before his interruption. Recognising the actress's character as that of the sickly and impoverished Mollser, the protestor put his coat over her to keep her warm. For Yeats, this was a hilarious and revealing indication of the obtuseness of republican anti-state militancy: what the protestor appeared not to notice was that Mollser and her illness and poverty were entirely fictional. 'She was not the actress in his eyes', japed Yeats in a letter to his friend Sir Herbert Grierson on 21 February 1926, 'but the consumptive girl' (*The Letters of W.B. Yeats*, 1954, p. 711).

Yeats' remarks show how the conventions of theatre can be called upon to shore up the commonsense nature of certain political norms. Acceptable political action is defined as a corollary of good behaviour in the theatre: not 'rioting' by climbing onto the stage but sitting peacefully in the auditorium and delegating imaginative authority to the actors on stage, who are clearly understood to be fictional. By this standard, an institutional national theatre becomes a way of maintaining the vitally important distinction between play-acting and real life, between theatrical and non-theatrical action. Before, during and after Ireland's political independence, in other words, Ireland's national theatre functioned as an institution that didn't just perform plays; it was also a place that worked in support of the idea that the only legitimate form of political action was that which abided by the representative conventions of parliamentary democracy. In Ireland, very conspicuously, the theatre is never just about theatre; it is also about ratifying norms of behaviour that underpin our conception of what constitutes 'normal' political and social action. I have argued that the reason this is especially visible in Ireland is that Ireland is a country where such norms have been persistently challenged by an often-brutal history of colonisation and colonial injustice and by violent guerrilla warfare and resistance. In delimiting the ability to act and to intervene in society, Irish theatre contributes to a system of control that is so powerful it operates with the same kind of invisible omnipresence that the Italian Marxist thinker Antonio Gramsci describes as hegemony. Irish theatre is hegemonic, that is, because it conveys a powerful impression that there are strict boundaries to what constitutes proper political action. The ability to act and intervene in any political or social situation is presented largely as a matter of trusting in our representatives, whether they are standing on stage or sitting in parliament. This is more of an exercise in sublimation than one of acting up.

Nevertheless, just because a play is written according to a naturalistic dramaturgy or for a national theatre does not mean that it is conservative or without any subversive political effect. *The Plough and the Stars* and *Juno and the Paycock* may well show all forms of political militancy as misguided, but these plays are also mordantly critical of the bourgeois religious and social pieties of the new postcolonial state. The Irish state may have approved of O'Casey's anti-republican views, but it also reacted angrily to the scene in *The Plough* where the Irish flag is shown in a public house, and in the same space as a prostitute. Moreover, the closing moments of *Juno*, in which the drunken Boyle and Joxer shuffle and stumble about on a bare stage, and of *The Plough*, where two English soldiers sip tea and sing nostalgically about home (while Dublin burns), encapsulate a naturalism that has been stretched to breaking point. With the way in which these scenes give emphasis to stage imagery over narrative action and to social disintegration, O'Casey's plays finish at a place not so very far from the point at which Beckett's plays begin.

Another example of the subversive effects of naturalism – this time from the 1930s – is provided by the dramatist Teresa Deevy. Written during a period when the Irish state deployed a panoply of legislative measures to control women's sexuality and restrict women's access to the public sphere, Deevy's *King of Spain's Daughter* (Abbey Theatre, Dublin, 1935) and *Katie Roche* (Abbey Theatre, Dublin, 1936) present Abbey Theatre audiences with vivaciously sexualised and unruly female protagonists (Annie in *King of Spain* and Katie in *Katie Roche*). Trapped within the brutalising and coercive norms of Irish patriarchy, Deevy's defiant women are torn between conceptions of marriage as a romantic fantasy and as a lifelong imprisonment. The action of Deevy's plays is naturalistic, certainly, but it is also characterised by features (such as the 'No traffic' and 'Road closed' signs at the beginning of *King of Spain's Daughter*) that owe much to expressionism. For Deevy, as for O'Casey, Brendan Behan, Murphy and Friel, 'natural' behaviour is shown as textured by conventionality and social performance.

Theatre outside the theatre 2

Loren Kruger's seminal 1990 work on national theatres *The National Stage: Theatre and Cultural Legitimation in England, France, and America* laments the assumption that national representation in the theatre and national representation in politics are always inextricably and beneficially connected (p. 6). What is overlooked, she complains, is not only the idea of theatre as a site of contestation but the existence of competing, multiple and counter-publics – groups of people whose political interests are such that they find themselves organised against the interests of the state. Kruger's argument is that national theatres tend to function to consolidate a particular dominant way of thinking about politics and that this rules counter-publics out of consideration.

But as anyone who has experienced the exuberant and often carnival-like atmosphere of a protest march will recognise, the theatrical is of crucial importance. It is important because the very existence of a counter-public depends on the idea of transformation: a counter-public is, almost by definition, committed to an inversion of prevailing, commonsense logics. When a counter-public expresses itself by means of a performance, what takes place can be quite extraordinary and often not like theatre at all. It can appear to make little sense because it violates the naturalistic axiom that every action must have a motive. To this extent, the performative and cultural manifestations of a counter-public are either not recognised at all or are viewed as scandalous, absurd and sometimes abhorrent. As one example of this, let's consider the 'dirty protests' in Northern Ireland in 1979–80.

The no-wash, or dirty, protests took place in those sections of Northern Ireland prisons dedicated to the incarceration of Irish republicans (members of the IRA and other republican paramilitary groups). They began as the escalation of a series of earlier protests that had taken place since 1976 in response to the British government's insistence that republican prisoners must wear prison uniforms. This insistence was highly charged because these prisoners had previously been granted 'special category' status – a status that recognised the political nature of the conflict in Northern Ireland and the political motivation of the prisoners. Before 1976, in other words, republican inmates had been treated as political prisoners – in effect as prisoners of war – and had been allowed to wear their own clothes. To the British government's move towards a policy of criminalisation, republican prisoners responded by refusing to wear prison garb. Naked, the prisoners occupied their cells with no form of covering except a blanket. The blanket became a distinctive costume, and the prisoners were soon known as 'the blanket men'. They were supported by regular solidarity marches in Irish and English cities, often led by individuals (sometimes the mothers of prisoners) who were themselves wearing blankets. The protests by the blanket men escalated following complaints by prisoners that prison officers repeatedly beat them when they left their cells to take a shower, to slop out or to walk to the lavatories. These protests began in March 1978 and entailed prisoners first refusing to wash and slop out their cells and then covering the walls of their cells with faeces and urine. They ended with another, more deadly and better-known protest: the hunger strikes of 1980–81. Steve McQueen's recent film *Hunger* (2008) offers a striking account of these actions.

The blanket and no-wash protests introduced into the prisons a dynamic of performance. In addition to an expression of the vulnerability and oppression of the Northern Ireland nationalist minority, the blanket men and especially the dirty protest offered a strikingly ironic performance of barbarity. It was as if the prisoners were deliberately evoking the colonial paradigm that the policy of criminalisation was designed to efface and repudiate. Barbarism as the antithesis of a colonial civilising state represented by the institution of the prison was an opposition that the prisoners deliberately and graphically performed. Instead of performing the submission, abjection and despair that the prison regime had sought to impose on the prisoners by compelling them to wear uniforms and comply with the regime in the new purpose-built prison of Long Kesh (or 'The Maze'), prisoners smeared their cell walls with their own waste, thereby conjuring a horrific image of something repressed, non-conforming and recalcitrant to any colonial project of civility. It was an action that was so stark and so appalling that it seemed to demand intervention from the spectator. This is a little like confronting a theatre audience with exactly what it finds most uncomfortable and disconcerting but also – and after reflection – revealing. To this extent, the Northern Ireland dirty protests can be related to a very different kind of performance context: the anti-pornography acts of U.S. performance artists Annie Sprinkle and Karen Finley, in which the voyeuristic fantasies involved in a tradition of male spectatorship are thrown back on the spectator when, for example, he is invited to gaze through a speculum at Sprinkle's cervix or is confronted by a naked Finley performing an out-of-control female body (for more on this, see Rebecca Schneider's *The Explicit Body in Performance*, 1997).

In any case, the dirty protests invested spectatorship – normally conceived of as disinterested – with an ethical imperative. In *Formations of Violence* (1991), anthropologist Allen Feldman argues that the logic underlying the dirty protests was an attempt by the prisoners to expose the inhumanity of the state by means of a kind of 'deflating mimesis' (p. 236). Excreta-covered cell walls were turned into a mise en scène that exposed the incarceratory tactics of the state as brutal and unjust and that evoked – albeit ironically – the colonial stereotype of the barbaric and undisciplined Irishman. What the prisoners were doing was using a performance of abnegation to turn punishment into protest (see Leila Neti's 2003 essay 'Blood and Dirt', p. 77). The prisoners' refusal of prison clothing and especially the refusal of shame attached to smearing faeces on the walls of their cells were ways of throwing shame back on the prison system.

The performances of the dirty protests of Northern Ireland involved a free and loose way of thinking about the body. This way of thinking resembles that adopted by an actor or performer when he or she walks on stage. In both cases, the body is thought of almost as something external to oneself, as a malleable instrument not bound inevitably and for all time to a particular mode of behaviour or socialisation, as a mimetic tool capable of independent expression and performance. One of the radical (if unintended) consequences of this way of thinking about the body is that it destabilises, or threatens to destabilise, the ways in which we think about gender and sexual identity. Although unintended, this was an important effect of the dirty protests, particularly when female republican prisoners undertook a similar action. The writer Margaretta D'Arcy, who briefly took part in the dirty protest, describes how the menstrual blood on the cell walls in Armagh women's prison was regarded by nationalists as a source of almost unspeakable shame and embarrassment and was never discussed in any of the official organs of the republican movement (*Tell Them Everything*, 1981, p. 80). Menstrual blood was destabilising because it was an indictment not just of the brutality of the state and its colonial history but of the same patriarchal codes that were shared by most in the republican movement as well. From this perspective it is possible to consider the hunger strikes that followed the dirty protest as a major change of direction, that is, as a pulling back from the radical transgressiveness that the dirty protests managed – albeit inadvertently – to expose. For anthropologist Begoña Aretxaga, in *Shattering Silence* (1997), 'menstrual blood became a symbol through which gender identity was reflected, pushing to the surface what had been otherwise erased' (p. 139). What happens with a hunger strike, on the other hand, is a closing up of the body's orifices and a shutting down – finally and altogether – of the body as an instrument of performance. Significantly, what also happened in the case of the Northern Ireland hunger strike was a return to traditional systems of representation in the sense that women were not allowed to participate in the strike (David Beresford, *Ten Men Dead*, 1994, pp. 74 and 79), and male hunger strikers were chosen from a pool of volunteers according to the region they came from and the implications of this for constitutional politics.

What I have been suggesting in this section is that the meaning of some protests – particularly those that either appear to be or are presented as bizarre – can often be discerned when they are regarded as forms of theatrical representation. Insisting that theatrical performance takes place both inside and outside theatre buildings is important because it encourages us to view theatre as plural and because it allows us to see that political actions can be wildly heterogeneous.

Modernity

In each of the previous sections one general point recurs: as an institution, the theatre in Ireland is fundamentally bound up with anxieties about being modern. This is as true for the Irish theatre's seventeenth-century beginnings under the patronage of the English Lord Deputy as it is for today's state-sponsored and business-friendly Abbey Theatre. For colonialism, as for the mainstream nationalisms that succeed it, the theatre's primary cultural function is to modernise a society that needs to catch up. In Ireland, speeding up in order to catch up is a deep-rooted cultural habit. This is hardly surprising given that the message of colonialism is that the modern is always somewhere else, always slipping away from the native's tantalised grasp, always something that must be striven for with special zeal. As the Indian historian and theorist Dipesh Chakrabarty points out in his 2002 book *Habitations of Modernity*, the fervent secularism of the modern – setting its face against what it sees as the absurdly retarding forces of the religious and the traditional – is even more zealous in the case of a country that has been colonised (pp. 20–37). In Ireland, the task of having the theatre champion secular modernity tends to be viewed as so urgent and important that it overrides any sense of other potential functions for a theatre – particularly those associated with opening up worlds of repressed desire and utopian possibility. An impression of what this means in practice can be gained from a brief survey of recent Irish drama.

One major idea in Irish plays from the 1980s to the present is that Ireland has to choose between two modes of expression: between a bizarre, backward-looking and almost exclusively rural premodernity often portrayed as gothic grotesquery and an identity based on speed, sexual attractiveness and an amazing, almost acrobatic, ability to compromise and adjust. The conclusion of Brian Friel's 1980 watershed play *Translations* (Guildhall, Derry, 1980), for example, leaves its audience in little doubt regarding Ireland's stark choice for the future: between the IRA-like guerrilla activities of militant anti-colonial resistance (the course of action adopted by the Donnelly twins, Doalty, and perhaps Owen) and a more cautious and urbane process of adaptation proposed in the final scene by the play's schoolteacher, Hugh. Whereas the option of militancy is seen as repeating a cycle of violent attacks and retaliation remarkably similar to what was then taking place in Northern Ireland, the schoolteacher's option is based on compromise and accommodation. The English language must be accepted and learnt, Hugh proposes, even if it may not be fully adequate to the subtleties of interpersonal exchanges – what Friel describes as the task of interpreting 'between privacies' (p. 308). It is not difficult for a thinking audience to discern which of these is the better option. In the sense that no other peaceable alternative is presented, Friel's play advocates an acceptance of the political and economic status quo (British imperial power) and of a process of retrieving identity through culture. In addition, the play's trajectory moves the audience to accept that a society cannot reproduce itself without recognising certain fundamental truths, the most basic of which is the patriarchal domestic unit – what Hugh refers to elliptically as 'the need for our own' (p. 307). Friel's challenging wisdom is a rejection of the shibboleths of republican heroism in the name of a more pragmatic understanding of the centrality of the family and the home. Ireland as a goddess is replaced by the subordinate, ameliorating figure of the wife and mother.

Fighting back, politicising the Irish language and arguing that the conflict in Northern Ireland can best be resolved through militant political or paramilitary action is presented as dangerously misguided. Even though the first production of *Translations* in Derry's Guildhall received a standing ovation on its opening night – with nationalist and unionist politicians applauding together – this is a play that is resolutely opposed to any radical political change. What it advocates is an acceptance of the reality of British state power in Northern Ireland, the recognition of nationalist cultural identity in Northern Ireland and a substantial lowering of nationalist political expectations.

The political mood conveyed by *Translations* in 1980 was a signal of what was to follow. It is not so much a political quietism that is extolled and sometimes celebrated in Irish drama over the next three decades but Ireland's virtually gymnastic ability to adjust to whatever the state and global capitalism require of it. Lowering political demands – almost to the point of evanescence – is the order of the day. Clinging to tradition (particularly Roman Catholic, rural or nationalist tradition) and slowness or reluctance to change in the face of capitalist exigencies are seen as forms of myopic impoverishment and as neuroses that teeter, dangerously, on the brink of the psychotic. The plays of Martin McDonagh provide the best and also the most extreme example of this point. Lightweight, farcical and cruelly dismissive of what they portray as rural backwaters, McDonagh's award-winning and widely produced plays depict as bizarre and incomprehensible anything that has not caught up with the intoxicating world of modernity. What a play such as *The Beauty Queen of Leenane* (Town Hall Theatre, Galway, 1996) encourages is a further widening of the existential gulf between our world as cosmopolitan theatre spectators and the benighted world of the characters on stage. This is evident in the marked anachronisms of the play's setting, with its kitchen-cum-living room decorated with a crucifix and framed picture of John and Robert Kennedy. The play's two main characters are also described in a manner that sets them off from the audience. As through a distorting mirror, what we are presented with on stage is an undisciplined, black-and-white vision of the Irish past: Maureen, 'a plain, slim woman of about forty', and her near-senile mother, Mag Folan, 'a stoutish woman in her early seventies with short, tightly permed grey hair and a mouth that gapes slightly' (p. 1).

From this beginning little changes. After Maureen's discovery that her incontinent mother has deliberately sabotaged her once-in-a-blue-moon chance to escape this stultifying atmosphere through a romance with an emigrating local man, Maureen retaliates by clamping her mother's hand to the red-hot iron surface of a cooking range, pouring boiling cooking oil over it, throwing boiling oil over her mother's torso and face and, finally, beating Mag's skull in with a poker. The play ends with Maureen drifting into the same senility as her mother: in McDonagh's world there is no hope for this blighted rural dystopia. Allusions in the opening scene to 'the English stealing our language, and our land, and our God knows what' (p. 5) and to the effects of anti-Irish racism in Britain are made by the play not as factors that require any serious consideration but as further evidence (if evidence were needed) of the farcical irrelevance of these characters' terms of reference. For McDonagh, evoking the legacies of Ireland's colonial history is about as gauche and as anachronistic as decorating your living room with a crucifix or hanging a picture of the Kennedys.

Another way of looking at *The Beauty Queen of Leenane* – a play that won four Tony awards in 1998 – is that it presents the theatre audience with a stage vision of what the alternative to Ireland's Celtic Tiger modernity might look like. It looks bad: thick headed, ugly, amoral, violent. *The Beauty Queen of Leenane* offers us 'Irish' in its adjectival and colonial sense: as a sequence of actions and characters that appear bizarre, exotic, violent, comically entertaining and – crucially – without any ethical framework of their own. When news of the priest's suicide reaches Valene and Coleman, the main characters of *The Lonesome West* (Town

Hall Theatre, Galway, 1997), Coleman comments, 'We shouldn't laugh', and then 'both pull a serious face' (p. 50). But this distancing response is exactly what is intended by McDonagh's plays. As a place of slowness, obstinacy and sexual frustration – 'the poleaxing boredom of Irish rural life' is how Michael Billington puts it in relation to *The Beauty Queen of Leenane* ('Synge-Song Fable of Galway Solitude', *Manchester Guardian Weekly*, 17 March 1996, Arts Section, p. 26) – McDonagh's rural Ireland needs to be abandoned, and quickly. If it can't be abandoned physically, then it can at least be abandoned culturally. That the theatre audience has already done one or both of these actions is what these plays' performances set out to confirm, enact and celebrate. Victor Merriman's assessment of McDonagh's plays, in his 2006 essay 'Decolonization Postponed', as neo-colonial apologies for the failures of Irish independence offers an astute summary: 'the repellent figures presented turn out to be representations of those most fully betrayed by indigenous self-rule; emigrants, undereducated peasants, bachelor smallholders, women abandoned in rural isolation by economic collapse' (pp. 274–75).

McDonagh's plays can be thought of alongside another 1990s theatrical phenomenon: *Riverdance*, first performed in Dublin as part of the Eurovision song contest in 1994. What is demonstrated by the speed and almost military conformity of the *Riverdance* dance troupe is that Irishness does not have to be benighted; it can instead be viewed as a performance of speed and pliancy. Even though the clichéd heterosexuality and slick physical conformity of the dancers appear quite the opposite of the tortured and dysfunctional physical attributes of McDonagh's characters, the overall effect is the same. Insofar as Irishness is important, it is important as a way of facilitating and speeding up the movement of global capital. As Aoife Monks argues in 'Comely Maidens and Celtic Tigers', *Riverdance* functions as a neo-colonial phenomenon and as a site of 'aspiration and fantasy in Irish popular culture' (p. 9). The *Riverdance* company itself – operating globally, with three troupes of dancers performing simultaneously in different countries – is an embodiment of this altogether celebratory perspective on Ireland's globalised market economy. Monks comments that Irishness 'becomes a performance on the part of the spectator, an opportunity to participate in a series of associations and pleasures attached to a cultural category, dislocated from time or space' (p. 14).

More latterly, it is Irishness itself that has come to be identified with Irish drama's ironising and distancing process. Indeed, being Irish today is so keenly postmodernist that you don't have to be Irish at all to be Irish. As in *Riverdance* and the plays of Martin McDonagh, Irishness is transformed into the act of performing one's distance not just from Ireland's famous and much-trumpeted benighted past but also from *all* systems of ethical attachment (cultural, political, religious) that have been, are or could be associated with Ireland. Ethical and religious allegiances, in particular, are derided. The experience of *Riverdance*, for example, makes us feel that what connects us to Ireland consists of a combination of verifying stylistic details (signifiers such as white skin, certain rhythmical dance moves and recognisable place names and localities) and a state of being that is sceptical about and dismissive of the specificities of Irish history and amazingly amenable and pliant with respect to the needs of a global capitalist future. Livened up with Spanish flamenco and American tap dance, *Riverdance* is about demonstrating, physically and almost literally, that Irishness is a state of being: a state of being that involves not just throwing shapes but a euphoric bending over backwards to meet the needs of a global market. We belong to Ireland, such works suggest, by virtue of our ability to speed up and keep distance from its troublesome history, and this is just as true for those living in Ireland as it is for those who do not. In his 2002 essay 'Speed Limits', cultural critic Michael Cronin describes this process as 'a war against time' and relates this obsession with speed and global integration to a cultural preoccupation with not remembering (p. 65). In the context of Irish theatre I am suggesting that there is a dominant trend that involves an emptying out of all ethical attachments to a country and a history (as opposed to a state) and a full-scale, no-holds-barred embrace of compliance and adaptability. To this extent, performing Irishness as a state of moral and ethical scepticism provides an active support for the idea of Ireland as 'a competition state', the term used by political economist Peadar Kirby to describe a series of state-sponsored interventions designed to give precedence to the goals of economic competitiveness over those of social cohesion and welfare (*The Celtic Tiger in*

Distress, 2002, pp. 142–44; Kirby and Mary Murphy, 'Ireland as a "Competition State"', 2007, p. 3).

A similar idea of a deterritorialised Irishness – of Irishness without Ireland – is evident in the narrative action of plays by Conor McPherson, Enda Walsh and Eugene O'Brien. For these playwrights Irishness is a condition of repetition, hauntings and fascinating and irrational allegiances. Irishness betokens not so much a relationship to a particular place or to a particular history or politics but a relationship to deep-rooted, maimed psychological and psychic conditions. To this extent, plays such as McPherson's *The Weir* (Royal Court Theatre, London, 1997) or Walsh's *The Walworth Farce* (Town Hall Theatre, Galway, 2006) and *The New Electric Ballroom* (Town Hall Theatre, Galway, 2008) or O'Brien's *Eden* (Peacock Theatre, Dublin, 2001) present the idea of an unmodernised Ireland – persistently characterised by sexual and intellectual incoherence – as existing at a reassuringly long remove from the more self-aware and future-oriented world of the theatre audience.

Interestingly, this cluster of ideas is the specific concern of Marie Jones' *Stones in His Pockets* (Lyric Theatre, Belfast, 1999). The play's action takes place on a film set located 'at a scenic spot near a small village in Co. Kerry' and features two protagonists – Charlie Conlon and Jake Quinn – who also act all the other characters in the play. With improvisatory skill and theatrical panache, Jones' play explores the value and relevance of rural Ireland and its traditional agricultural economy to a contemporary world dominated by globalisation. Like Brian Friel's *Philadelphia,*

Here I Come! (Gaiety Theatre, Dublin, 1964) – also characterised by omniscient character-commentators – *Stones in His Pockets* suggests that those living in rural Ireland and committed to traditional values are faced with a choice that is not a choice: emigration and adjustment through performance or a suicidal attachment to a single identity. The one character in the play who fails to grasp the necessity of abandoning sentimental ideas of identity for the euphoria of role-playing is Séan Harkin; realising that he can neither maintain the traditional nor escape from it to Hollywood, Harkin drowns himself by walking into a lake with his pockets full of stones. Jones' play suggests that the only non-suicidal response to traditional Ireland is via the performative shifts and postmodernist adjustments of endless role-playing. This is evident not just in the play's narrative but in the virtuosity that is shown by two actors playing a total of fourteen characters, and by the franchising of the play in Europe, North America and Australia. As Patrick Lonergan argues incisively in *Theatre and Globalization* (2009), *Stones in His Pockets* is a celebration of capitalist entrepreneurialism (p. 13).

To my mind a very different form of theatre is offered in certain plays by Marina Carr. Although Carr also treats the subject matter of rural Ireland in plays such as *By the Bog of Cats* (Abbey Theatre, Dublin, 1998) and *The Mai* (Peacock Theatre, Dublin, 1994), the emphasis is not so much on Ireland's need for adaptability and accelerated modernisation as on the extraordinary value of a marginalised culture in illuminating the repressions and phobias of the present. Hester the settled traveller in *By the Bog of Cats* and Grandma Fraochlán in *The Mai* – described as coming from a remote Irish-speaking island in the west of Ireland – are dispossessed figures whose uncanny insights offer a resource of ethical and psychological commentary. Carr's plays are preoccupied with states of neurosis that are not presented as existing at a comfortable distance from the future-oriented world of the audience. Instead, the plays show neuroses and repressions as underlying behaviour that we think of as normal and familiar. For example, *By the Bog of Cats* deals with the centrality of the mother-daughter relationship and with the far-reaching consequences of its traumatic severing. The play's protagonist, Hester Swayne, is haunted by the memory of the mother who abandoned her – 'There's a longin' in me for her that won't quell this while gone' (p. 358) – and the play concludes with Hester killing her own daughter and then herself to ensure that this pattern is not repeated (p. 395). It is the very marginality and anomalous modernity of Carr's characters and, in particular, their rootedness in traditional Irish culture that offer them their resources of insight. Hester's status as a settled traveller allows her access to a way of thinking that is visionary and unconstrained. Far from confirming and celebrating the bourgeois conventions of the audience, Carr's plays suggest that it is exactly these conventions that need to be challenged insofar as they tend to conceal, simplify and distort the more complex realities of desire and repression. The wedding feast scene in *By the Bog of Cats* offers a brilliant example of this. Here Carr shows the groom and bride (Carthage Kilbride and Caroline Cassidy) sidelined not only by the role-playing of the ceremony itself but by the way in which the theatricality of the occasion allows the groom's mother (Mrs Kilbride) to express desire for her son. Instead of presenting marginalised characters as hilariously redundant, Carr's *By the Bog of Cats* and *The Mai* achieve the opposite. These plays show how the marginal and the unmodern may also have a positive function: that of exposing the neuroses and trauma that, so frequently, underlie our conceptions of the normal.

One of Irish theatre's main preoccupations is the way in which behaviour that appears ordinary and natural and quotidian also appears at times to be a social performance. Like the use of the word 'Irish' as a verb, this strong sense of the histrionic is a way of refusing to be tied down to the 'facts' of a situation and of evoking perspectives on the world that are vivaciously exaggerated and bizarrely revelatory. Performativity does indeed have many pejorative and enduring associations with the historical condition of being irish; nevertheless, and just like the theatre itself, it can also suggest a greatly expanded conception of what can be done in, to and for the world. Perhaps a reputation for acting a part is not so bad after all, especially when you consider that the most important thing about acting a role is that it demonstrates a capacity for acting up and acting differently. Moreover, thinking of Irish culture as richly performative could also mean realising a culture's deep resources for resistance and for fun. In today's atmosphere of recession and right-wing political and economic conformity, the resources of theatre and performance may help us imagine new ways of acting and may encourage an openness to more helpful and liberating ways of imagining the future. Never were such ways more badly needed.

further reading

Irish theatre studies is now a major critical field, and many articles and monographs are published each year. The best selection of modern (post-1899) Irish plays can be found in John Harrington's *Modern and Contemporary Irish Drama* (2nd edition), and an indispensable book on Irish theatre history in general is Christopher Morash's *A History of Irish Theatre 1601–2000*. Some indication of the rich native traditions of performance can be found in the meticulous, groundbreaking scholarship of Alan Fletcher, in Helen Burke's 'Country Matters', and in the works by Alan Gailey, Pádraigín Ní Uallacháin, Gearóid Ó Crualaoich and Mark Phelan listed below. The best overview of the preoccupations of twentieth-century Irish drama remains Nicholas Grene's incisive study *The Politics of Irish Drama*. Other, non-institutional forms of performance are discussed in Burke's *Riotous Performances* and in the works by Sara Brady and Fintan Walsh, Joan Fitzpatrick Dean, James Moran, Phelan and Paige Reynolds in this list; however, only Burke and Phelan deal with pre-twentieth-century theatre. For the eighteenth century, the work of Burke and Christopher J. Wheatley is indispensable; Burke's work, in particular, offers an extraordinary exemplum of cultural criticism and theatre history at its best. For critical approaches that emphasise issues such as class, the role of the state, colonialism and globalisation, see the works listed for Adrian Frazier (on the Abbey Theatre), Patrick Lonergan, Victor Merriman, Phelan, Pilkington, and Paul Murphy. For critical perspectives that focus more on the achievements of Irish drama, see Anthony Roche's *Contemporary Irish Drama* and Christopher Murray's *Twentieth-Century Irish Drama*. The publications by political economist Peadar Kirby cited here offer a succinct and trenchantly critical account of Ireland's economic policies before, during and after its years as the Celtic Tiger.

Allen, Nicholas. *Modernism, Ireland and Civil War*. Cambridge: Cambridge UP, 2009.

Aretxaga, Begoña. *Shattering Silence: Women, Nationalism and Political Subjectivity in Northern Ireland*. Princeton, NJ: Princeton UP, 1997.

Arnold, Matthew. From 'On the Study of Celtic Literature' [1867]. *Poetry and Ireland Since 1800: A Source Book*. Ed. Mark Storey. London: Routledge, 1988. 61–68.

Barnes, Clive. 'Critic's Notebook: Comments, Not Complaints, about Broadway, Mr. Papp and the Irish'. *New York Times* 8 December 1976: 75.

Barrett, W. 'Irish Drama.' *New Ireland Review* March–August 1895: 38–41.

Beckett, Samuel. *The Letters of Samuel Beckett 1929–1940*. Ed. Martha Dow Fehsenfeld and Lois More Overbeck. Cambridge: Cambridge UP, 2009.

Beresford, David. *Ten Men Dead: The Story of the Irish Hunger Strike.* London: HarperCollins, 1994.

Bhabha, Homi. *The Location of Culture.* London: Routledge, 1994.

Billington, Michael. 'Synge-Song Fable of Galway Solitude.' Arts Section. *Manchester Guardian Weekly* 17 March 1996: 26.

Boucicault, Dion. *Selected Plays of Dion Boucicault.* Chosen and introduced by Andrew Parkin. Gerrards Cross, UK: Colin Smythe, 1987.

Brady, Sara, and Fintan Walsh. *Crossroads: Performance Studies and Irish Culture.* Basingstoke, UK: Palgrave Macmillan, 2009.

Bratton, Jacky. *New Readings in Theatre History.* Cambridge: Cambridge UP, 2003.

Brennan, Helen. *The Story of Irish Dance.* Dingle, Co. Kerry: Brandon, 1999.

Burke, Helen. 'The Revolutionary Prelude: The Dublin Stage in the Late 1770s and Early 1780s.' *Eighteenth-Century Life* 22 (1998): 7–18.

———. *Riotous Performances: The Struggle for Hegemony in the Irish Theater, 1712–1784.* Notre Dame, IN: U of Notre Dame P, 2003.

———. 'Teague and the Ethnicization of Labor in Early Modern British Culture.' *Eighteenth-Century Theory and Interpretation* 46.3 (2005): 237–44.

———. 'Acting in the Periphery.' *The Cambridge Companion to British Theatre 1730–1830.* Ed. Jane Moody and Daniel O'Quin. Cambridge: Cambridge UP, 2007. 219–31.

———. 'Country Matters: Irish "Waggery" and the Irish and British Theatrical Traditions.' *Players, Playwrights, Playhouses: Investigating Performance, 1660–1800.* Ed. Michael Cordner and Peter Holland. Basingstoke, UK: Palgrave Macmillan, 2007. 213–28.

Carr, Marina. *By the Bog of Cats. Modern and Contemporary Irish Drama.* Ed. John P. Harrington. 2nd ed. New York: Norton, 2009. 352–97.

Chakrabarty, Dipesh. *Habitations of Modernity: Essays in the Wake of Subaltern Studies.* With a foreword by Homi K. Bhabha. Chicago, IL: U of Chicago P, 2002.

Chambers, Lillian, and Eamonn Jordan, eds. *The Theatre of Martin McDonagh: A World of Savage Stories.* Dublin: Carysfort, 2006.

Cleary, Joe. 'Towards a Materialist-Formalist History of Twentieth-Century Irish Literature.' *Boundary 2* 31.1 (2004): 207–42. [Spec. iss., *Contemporary Irish Culture and Politics*]

Conley, Carolyn. 'The Agreeable Recreation of Fighting.' *Journal of Social History* 33.1 (1999): 57–72.

Cronin, Michael. 'Speed Limits: Ireland, Globalisation and the War against Time.' *Reinventing Ireland: Culture, Society and the Global Economy.* Ed. Peadar Kirby, Luke Gibbons and Michael Cronin. London: Pluto, 2002. 54–68.

D'Arcy, Margaretta. *Tell Them Everything: A Sojourn in the Prison of Her Majesty Queen Elizabeth II at Ard Macha (Armagh).* London: Pluto, 1981.

Dean, Joan Fitzpatrick. *Riot and Great Anger: Stage Censorship in the Twentieth Century.* London: U of Wisconsin P, 2004.

Deevy, Teresa. *Three Plays: Katie Roche, The King of Spain's Daughter, The Wild Goose.* London: Macmillan, 1939.

Fanon, Frantz. *The Wretched of the Earth.* London: Penguin, 1967.

Feldman, Allen. *Formations of Violence: The Narrative of the Body and Political Terror in Northern Ireland.* Chicago, IL, and London: U of Chicago P, 1991.

Finfacts. 'Comment: UN Human Development Report 2004 – Irish Richer Than Americans; Second in Poverty Index.' October 2004. 30 November 2009 <www.finfacts.com/comment/unhumandevel-opmentreportirelandcomment18.htm>.

Fletcher, Alan J. *Drama, Performance, and Polity in Pre-Cromwellian Ireland.* Cork: Cork UP, 2000.

———. *Drama and the Performing Arts in Pre-Cromwellian Ireland: Sources and Documents from the Earliest Times until c. 1642.* Cambridge: D.S. Brewer, 2001.

Foster, R. F. *Modern Ireland 1600–1972.* London: Penguin, 1988.

Frazier, Adrian. *Behind the Scenes: Yeats, Horniman, and the Abbey Theatre.* Berkeley: U of California P, 1990.

Friel, Brian. *Translations. Modern and Contemporary Irish Drama.* Ed. John P. Harrington. 2nd ed. New York: Norton, 2009. 255–308.

Gailey, Alan. *Irish Folk Drama.* Cork: Mercier, 1969.

Glassie, Henry. *All Silver and No Brass: An Irish Christmas Mumming.* Dublin: Dolmen, 1976.

Gregory, Augusta. *Our Irish Theatre: A Chapter of Autobiography by Lady Gregory.* Gerrards Cross, UK: Colin Smythe, 1972.

Grene, Nicholas. *The Politics of Irish Drama: Plays in Context from Boucicault to Friel.* Cambridge: Cambridge UP, 1999.

Harrington, John, ed. *Modern and Contemporary Irish Drama*. 2nd ed. New York: Norton, 2009.

Harris, Peter. 'Chronological Table of Plays Produced in London (1920–2006).' *Irish Theatre in England*. Ed. Richard Cave and Ben Levitas. Dublin: Carysfort, 2007. 195–286.

Harris, Susan Cannon. *Gender and Modern Irish Drama*. Bloomington: Indiana UP, 2002.

———. 'Mixed Marriage: Sheridan, Macklin, and the Hybrid Audience.' *Players, Playwrights, Playhouses: Investigating Performance, 1660–1800*. Ed. Michael Cordner and Peter Holland. Basingstoke, UK: Palgrave Macmillan, 2007. 189–212.

Herr, Cheryl, ed. *For the Land They Loved: Irish Political Melodramas 1890–1925*. Syracuse, NY: Syracuse UP, 1991.

Hitchcock, Robert. *An Historical View of the Irish Stage from the Earliest Period down to the Close of the Season 1788*. 2 vols. Dublin: William Folds, 1794.

Kearney, A. T. 'Ireland Clings to Top Global Spot.' *Foreign Policy* magazine Globalization Index. 24 February 2004. 22 August 2009 <www.foreignpolicy.com/story/cms.php?story_id=2523>.

Jones, Marie. *Stones in His Pockets*. London: Nick Hern, 2000.

Kennedy, David. 'The Ulster Region and the Theatre.' *Lagan* 4 (1946): 51–55.

Kettle, Tom. 'Mr Yeats and the Freedom of the Theatre'. *United Irishman* 15 November 1902: 2–3.

Kirby, Peadar. *The Celtic Tiger in Distress: Growth with Inequality in Ireland*. Basingstoke, UK: Palgrave Macmillan, 2002.

———. 'The Competition State – Lessons from Ireland.' *Limerick Papers in Politics and Public Administration* 1 (2009). <www.ul.ie/ppa/Politics/Kirby2009.pdf>.

———. *The Collapse of the Celtic Tiger*. Basingstoke, UK: Palgrave Macmillan, 2010.

Kirby, Peadar, and Mary Murphy, 'Ireland as a "Competition State".' *IPEG Papers in Global Political Economy* 28 (May 2007). <www.bisa-ipeg.org/papers/28%20Kirby%20and%20Murphy.pdf>.

Kruger, Loren. *The National Stage: Theatre and Cultural Legitimation in England, France, and America*. Chicago, IL: U of Chicago P, 1992.

Leeney, Cathy. 'Ireland's "Exiled" Women Playwrights: Teresa Deevy and Marina Carr.' *The Cambridge Companion to Twentieth-Century*

Irish Drama. Ed. Shaun Richards. Cambridge: Cambridge UP, 2004. 150–63.

Leeney, Cathy, and Anna McMullan. *The Theatre of Marina Carr: 'Before Rules Were Made.'* Dublin: Carysfort, 2003.

Levitas, Ben. *The Theatre of Nation: Irish Drama and Cultural Nationalism 1890–1916.* Oxford: Clarendon P, 2002.

Lloyd, David. *Ireland After History.* Cork: Cork UP, 1999.

Lonergan, Patrick. *Theatre and Globalization: Irish Drama in the Celtic Tiger Era.* Basingstoke, UK: Palgrave Macmillan, 2009.

Luckhurst, Mary. *'Lieutenant of Inishmore*: Selling (-Out) to the English'. *The Theatre of Martin McDonagh: A World of Savage Stories.* Ed. Lilian Chambers and Eamonn Jordan. Dublin: Carysfort, 2006. 116–29.

McDonagh, Martin. *The Beauty Queen of Leenane.* London: Methuen, 1996.

———. *The Lonesome West.* London: Methuen, 1997.

McMinn, Joseph. 'Swift and Theatre'. *Eighteenth-Century Ireland* 16 (2001): 35–46.

McMullan, Anna. 'Samuel Beckett's Theatre: Liminal Subjects and the Politics of Perception.' *Princeton University Library Chronicle* 68.1–2 (2006): 450–64.

Merriman, Victor. 'Staging Contemporary Ireland: Heartsickness and Hopes Deferred.' *The Cambridge Companion to Twentieth-Century Irish Drama.* Ed. Shaun Richards. Cambridge: Cambridge UP, 2004. 244–57.

———. 'Decolonization Postponed: The Theatre of Tiger Trash.' *The Theatre of Martin McDonagh: A World of Savage Stories.* Ed. Lilian Chambers and Eamonn Jordan. Dublin: Carysfort, 2006. 264–80.

Monks, Aoife. 'Comely Maidens and Celtic Tigers: *Riverdance* and Global Performance.' *Goldsmiths Performance Research Pamphlets* 1. London: U of London, 2007.

Moran, James. *Staging the Easter Rising: 1916 as Theatre.* Cork: Cork UP, 2005.

Morash, Christopher. *A History of Irish Theatre 1601–2000.* Cambridge: Cambridge UP, 2002.

———. 'Irish Theatre.' *The Cambridge Companion to Modern Irish Culture.* Cambridge: Cambridge UP, 2005. 322–38.

———. 'Theatre in Ireland, 1690–1800: From the Williamite Wars to the Act of Union.' *The Cambridge History of Irish Literature.*

Ed. Margaret Kelleher and Philip O'Leary. 2 vols. Cambridge: Cambridge UP, 2006. Vol. 1, 372–403.

Murphy, Paul. *Hegemony and Fantasy in Irish Drama, 1899–1949*. Basingstoke, UK: Palgrave Macmillan, 2008.

Murray, Christopher. *Twentieth-Century Irish Drama: Mirror up to Nation*. Manchester: Manchester UP, 1997.

Neti, Leila. 'Blood and Dirt: Politics of Women's Protest in Armagh Prison, Northern Ireland.' *Violence and the Body: Race, Gender and the State*. Ed. Arturo J. Aldama. Bloomington: Indiana UP, 2003. 77–93.

Ní Uallacháin, Pádraigín. *A Hidden Ulster: People, Songs and Traditions of Oriel*. Dublin: Four Courts, 2003.

Ó Crualaoich, Gearóid. 'The "Merry Wake".' *Irish Popular Culture 1650–1850*. Ed. J. S. Donnelly Jr and Kerby A. Miller. Dublin: Irish Academic P, 1998. 173–200.

O'Neill, Stephen. *Staging Ireland: Representations in Shakespeare and Renaissance Drama*. Dublin: Four Courts, 2007.

Ó Siadhail, Pádraig. *Stair Dhrámaíocht na Gaeilge*. Indreabhán, Conamara: Cló Iar-Chonnachta, 1993.

Ó Suilleabháin, Seán. *Irish Wake Amusements*. Cork: Mercier, 1967.

O'Toole, Fintan. *The Politics of Magic: The Work and Times of Tom Murphy*. Dublin: Raven Arts, 1987.

Phelan, Mark. 'Modernity, Geography and Historiography: (Re)-Mapping Irish Theatre History in the Nineteenth Century.' *The Performing Century: Nineteenth-Century Theatre's History*. Ed. Tracy C. Davis and Peter Holland. Basingstoke, UK: Palgrave Macmillan, 2007. 135–58.

Pilkington, Lionel. ' "The Superior Game": Colonialism and the Stereotype in Tom Murphy's *A Whistle in the Dark*.' *Ritual Remembering: History, Myth and Politics in Anglo-Irish Drama*. Ed. C. C. Barfoot and Rias van den Doel. Amsterdam: Rodopi, 1995. 165–79.

Pilkington, Lionel. 'Irish Theater Historiography and Political Resistance.' *Staging Resistance: Essays on Political Theater*. Ed. Jeanne Colleran and Jenny S. Spencer. Ann Arbor: Michigan UP, 1998. 13–30.

———. *Theatre and the State in Twentieth Century Ireland: Cultivating the People*. London and New York: Routledge, 2001.

———. 'The "Folk" and the Irish Theater: Re-reading J.M. Synge's *The Playboy of the Western World*.' *Princeton University Chronicle* 68.1–2 (2006–7): 295–305.

Reynolds, Paige. *Modernism, Drama, and the Audience for Irish Spectacle.*
    Cambridge: Cambridge UP, 2007.

Roche, Anthony. *Contemporary Irish Drama.* Basingstoke, UK: Palgrave
    Macmillan, 2009.

Schechner, Richard. 'Restoration of Behavior.' *Studies in Visual
    Communication* 7 (1981): 2.

Schneider, Rebecca. *The Explicit Body in Performance.* London and
    New York: Routledge, 1997.

Sweeney, Bernadette. *Performing the Body in Irish Theatre.* Basingstoke,
    UK: Palgrave Macmillan, 2008.

Synge, J. M. *The Playboy of the Western World. Modern and Contemporary
    Irish Drama.* Ed. John P. Harrington. 2nd ed. New York: Norton,
    2009. 68–112.

Toibin, Colm, ed. *Seeing Is Believing: Moving Statues in Ireland.*
    Mountrath, Co. Laois: Pilgrim, 1985.

Turner, Victor. *The History of the Theatres of London and Dublin.* 2 vols.
    London: T. Davies, 1761.

United Nations Development Programme. *Human Development Report
    2004: Cultural Liberty in Today's Diverse World.* 2004. 14 February
    2010 <http://hdr.undp.org/en/media/hdr04_complete.pdf>.
————. *Human Development Report 2005: International Cooperation at
    a Crossroads.* 2005. 30 November 2009 <http://hdr.undp.org/en/
    media/HDR05_complete.pdf>.

Watt, Stephen. *Joyce, O'Casey, and the Irish Popular Theater.* Syracuse, NY:
    Syracuse UP, 1991.

Wheatley, Christopher J. *Beneath Ïerne's Banners: Irish Protestant Drama of
    the Restoration and Eighteenth Century.* Notre Dame, IN: U of Notre
    Dame P, 1999.

Yeats, W. B. *The Letters of W.B. Yeats.* Ed. Allan Wade. London: Rupert
    Hart-Davis, 1954.
————. 'The Irish Literary Theatre' [1899]. *Uncollected Prose of W. B.
    Yeats: Volume 2, Reviews, Articles and Other Miscellaneous Prose.* Ed. J.
    P. Frayne and C. Johnson. London: Macmillan, 1975. 139–42.

index

acknowledgements

A big thank-you to series editor Jen Harvie for her extraordinary patience, fantastic encouragement, good humour and great ideas; to Kate Haines at Palgrave Macmillan for courtesy, understanding and useful suggestions; and to the book's two anonymous readers for their many helpful comments. Written during the wet summer of 2009, this book could easily have become a hard grind; that it didn't was due to the love, laughter and writing solidarity of Hélène Lecossois. Other indispensable sustenance came from the text, email and phone conversations with my friend Barra Ó Seaghdha and the invaluable company and support of my son Colin. For loans of books, hard-to-locate references, good advice and general buoyancy aids, I am grateful to my colleagues at the National University of Ireland, Galway: Adrian Frazier, Louis de Paor, Patrick Lonergan, Gearóid Ó Tuathaigh and Karen Walsh. Thank you also to Hugh Haughton, Padraig Lenihan, David Lloyd,

Mark Phelan and John David Rhodes, who, at different points in this book's genesis – and sometimes entirely without knowing it – provided intriguing pointers for further thinking and reading. Part of the analysis of *The Playboy of the Western World* appeared in the 2007–8 edition of the *Princeton University Library Chronicle*, and I am most grateful to its editor, Gretchen Oberfranc, for permission to republish.